MAGIC IN THE MOUNTAINS, THE YAKIMA SHAMAN: POWER & PRACTICE

by
Donald M. Hines

Great Eagle Publishing®

MAGIC IN THE MOUNTAINS, THE YAKIMA SHAMAN: POWER & PRACTICE

By Donald M. Hines

Published by: Great Eagle Publishing, Inc.
3020 Issaquah-Pine Lake Rd. SE
Suite 481
Issaquah, WA 98027-7255 U.S.A.

PUBLISHER'S CATALOGING IN PUBLICATION
(Prepared by Quality Books Inc.)

Hines, Donald Merrill, 1931-
Magic in the mountains, the Yakima shaman: power & practice/
Donald M. Hines.
　p. cm.
　Includes bibliographical references.
　ISBN 0-9629539-3-8

　1. Yakima Indians—Magic. 2. Yakima Indians—Medicine. 3. Shamans—United States. I. Title

E99.Y2H55 1993　299.7'84　　QBI93-759
Library of Congress Catalog Card Number: 93-078220

CONTENTS

PART ONE
PREFACE

PART TWO

Sapan-wuxit, Yakima Doctor (Click Relander 1900).
Smithsonian Institution photo 41-886-E

Ho-lite (Billy Sta-hai) ["Captain Billie"], leader in Dreamer Religion ceremonies, the Yakima tribe. April 1911. Historical Photograph Collections, Washington State University Libraries.

PART ONE

PREFACE

A. Shaman-Sorcerer-Physician

This is an exciting book because it reports of the Yakima Indian spirit-worker, or shaman. And from two perspectives: from only 17 years after the several tribes had been forced onto the reservation of the Confederated Tribes and Bands of the Yakima Indian Nation in 1855; and from the early years of this century when details of the Yakima shaman were recorded from these "medicine" men themselves. And this is an important book because the Yakima shamans themselves report of their magic, and of how they acquired and employed their powers. No white man can satisfactorily explain or theorize about the shaman and his works. But these shamans explained many of their practices to Yakima Valley Pioneer L.V. McWhorter, who faithfully recorded their words.

The Yakima Indians were superb supernaturalists, believers in ghosts, spirits—the power of magic. And the lore of the shaman and his practices was a significant element of Yakima tribal culture. By **shamanism** we mean ". . . all the practices by which supernatural power may be acquired by mortals, the exercise of that power either for good or evil, and all the concepts and beliefs associated with these practices."[1]

What makes this volume of lore about the Yakima shaman unique? First, included here are direct statements from shamans about how they acquired their powers, conducted their practices. And second, the lore is tribal specific. Indeed, these Yakima shamans reveal a strong sense of tribal identification not yet blurred by generations living within the area as well as cultural conflict that existed among the bands and tribes on the reservation. Finally, the shamanistic accounts arise from within an oral milieu—the tribes' languages had no written forms. Therefore, the "tellings" of the lore to McWhorter are so vital, yet so natural. And thanks to him, that lore was written down, and so is available to us today.

The shaman, the object of this volume, was but one of many roles as healer which an individual might fill. First, a Yakima shaman was a man or woman who had obtained one or more *tahmahnawis* (magical) spirit powers from an animal (perhaps an eagle, rattlesnake, or grizzly bear) while a youth. This individual began the exercise of his power as late as about age 40 when he undertook to heal not only disease, but also spirit possession from among his patients, and more. Second, a sorcerer was a shamanic individual who as a youth had received a destructive *tah* spirit, and was unable to control that spirit's bent to do great harm. Third, a physician was also present who was skilled at healing sickness, or injury. We cannot say that this physician's power derived from no *tahmahnawis* power.

B. Sources of the Data

The data used here were obtained from two sources. First, from 1872 - 1882, George Benson Kuykendall MD, was physician to the Yakima Agency located at Fort Simcoe, Washington Territory. His patients included reservation Indians and other individuals. According to Kuykendall, "soon after arriving at Fort Simcoe, Major Powell, of the Department of Ethnology in the Smithsonian Institution, at Washington, D.C., wrote me asking me to take up in behalf of the government, the study of Indian ethnology, language, folk lore [sic]; their myths, traditions and beliefs, and their ancient customs and usages."[2] Over the next ten years Kuykendall collected a large body of data some of which he published in 1889. We have no information on his methods of data collection. His papers were subsequently placed in the Special Collections, Holland Library, at Washington State University, Pullman.

Second, in 1903 Lucullus Virgil McWhorter moved from Ohio to "North Yakima" in the vicinity of the Yakima Indian Reservation. The purpose of his move west was to be close to Indian life. He brought with him his prize-winning herd of Devon cattle and continued his career as a cattle rancher. He promptly began the serious study and written record of the areas' Indian cultures, especially their oral traditions. He made many warm and active friendships with Yakimas with whom he hunted and camped, and visited with in his home. He participated in many tribal ceremonials, was adopted into the Yakima tribe, and was given several names including "Old Wolf" (*He-Mene-Ka-Wan*), "Big Foot, "Owl" or *Show-Paw-*

Tan, and others, names which McWhorter often used in his voluminous correspondence, and which he also mentioned on a program aired over KOIN-radio, Portland, Oregon, on 13 Jan 1943.

Until his death in 1944 McWhorter continued to collect Yakima lore and culture which he perceived was already fading from tribal memories. His collecting techniques were largely self-taught. He patterned his collecting methods after the bare outlines of collecting particulars obtained from the Bureau of American Ethnology, found subsequently in his papers. Commonly, he collected narratives heard around a campfire after a hunt, or in the longhouse—in proper context. McWhorter would listen, and then as soon after as possible would write down from memory the narratives which he had heard. Or, his Indian friends wrote down translations in English for numerous tribal narratives. McWhorter sought to be accurate, detailed, and thorough. He did not rewrite tales into literary forms such as the short story. But he often appended to tales his questions and an informant's answers which explained numerous details of the narratives, or he cited story details shared by other narratives. What is of critical importance—McWhorter collected and added to his files all sorts of Yakima narratives—from a myth to a legend to a magical belief—and more. No practiced folklorist, he knew little of the conventional genres and when to stop collecting; so he collected all that he heard. And he collected in depth as best he knew how—his labors comprise a priceless legacy of traditional oral lore and life from the Yakima nation.

At McWhorter's death in 1944, his papers, his

life's work, were given to then State College of Washington [W.S.U.]. McWhorter's son, Virgil, spent most of a year laboring to arrange his father's papers into proper order. Then the papers were placed into large gray file boxes—several hundred thousand items: books, clippings, journals, letters, photographs, notes, manuscripts, manuscript fragments, and mementos. Now, under the scholarly direction of Mr. John Guido, Head, Manuscripts, Archives and Special Collections, Holland Library at W.S.U., the papers continue to be consulted by numerous individuals.

C. Locale and the Culture

Until 1855 the Yakimas ranged over about 10,800,000 acres of Central Washington, especially along the Yakima River. In May 1855 the Yakima Reservation was created, comprising less than 1,400,000 acres. And placed on this reservation were some fourteen separate but closely related tribes and bands. According to Kuykendall, these included the Yakima, Palouse, Satus, Klikitat, *Pasquouse*, *Nen'atshapam*, *Klinguit*, *Kow-was-say-se*, *Li-ay-was*, *Skinpah*, *Wisham*, *Skyiks* [*Shyiks?*], *Ochecotes-Hamiltpa*, *Scapcat*.[3] In a census of 1910 some 1,262 Yakimas were counted.

Originally fishermen of the annual runs of salmon and of steelhead, tribesmen also hunted deer and other animals. And the tribeswomen collected roots and berries, air-dried the salmon as food stores against the long winter months. From along the Yakima River and ranging westward toward the Cascade Range, and northward toward present-day country of the *Wenatchees*, tribal hunters sought mountain sheep and goat, even bear.

The establishment of the reservation brought many changes. According to McWhorter in his time, beside traditional shamanism, forms of religion found on the reservation included Christian worship as missionized by the Roman Catholics and Methodists and others, the Native American Shaker church, and *Smohallah* worship.

D. Stages of the Shaman's Career

Training: The shaman's power was acquired early, but apparently employed at a late date. To begin with, a youth [boy or girl] might begin to "train" or to "prepare for a spirit experience early, age six to twelve. A youth . . . was sent out at night to some distant lonely place, to a lake, the mountains, the river, a large grove of trees, or some big rock pile. This was always at a considerable distance from home, a place usually quite unfrequented."[4] An old man might direct the youth's experience. For example, *Sam-a-lee-sack* [Salmon La Sac] ". . .was often employed by the Indian parents to guide, correct and even punish refractory children. For this purpose he sometimes made the journey from the Ellensburg Country to the Yakima Reservation. He would make the youngsters go into the icy waters of a creek or river on a cold winter morning, keeping them there with the aid of a keen switch. After a few moments the naked child was permitted to run into the tepee or house where, well-wrapped in blankets by a hot fire, he soon forgot the chilly bath of the morning."[5] Likewise, at perhaps modern Snow Lake, Salmon La Sac would tether self-willed and disobedient boys and girls there overnight.

But the lake was dreaded, shunned; with strange noises to be heard in the night. Even to look at the source of the noises was to invite death.[6]

Acquisition of Spirit Power (*Tahmahnawis*).

According to Spier, *Wishram Ethnography*, p. 240, at about age 12, a boy or girl would be taken to spend one or more nights at a remote spot. With no food or water, the youth was not to sleep, but was given a task to do such as heaping up a pile of stones. The youth might be sent again and again at each of several spots so that he or she might receive a spirit power. "The child knew nothing of what he was to expect, nor did the one who sent him on the quest. While he was sitting awaiting it, as in a dream the spirit animal approached in various guises: with a roaring sound, accompanied by flashes of fire, a high wind, hail and rain. The youth seeking shaman's power saw the animal, heard words spoken by this animal. He dreamt that the power spoke like a human: 'When some one is sick, you will cure him; you must then follow me singing.' The acquisition [of spirit power] was looked on as more or less involuntary." The spirit animal [sometimes a youth would obtain more than one spirit] would teach the youth a song, and more, and then disappear. With morning the youth would return to his or her village, but say little or nothing of the "spirit experience."[7]

Proclaiming Shamanic Power: After some period of time, the youth [even middle-aged man or woman] participated in a Shaman's Inaugural Dance to proclaim his shamanic power and to inaugurate his career. According to Spier, "then the boy tried

his power. He called out: 'Who is sick?' Someone came forward and lay down. He [neophyte shaman] sucked the spot, singing; others were dancing and singing, too, to help him. He took out the sickness, held it in his hand; black matter ran from it. He swallowed it to feed his spirit."[8]

Shamanic Healing: Shamanic cures were effected by the extraction of a foreign substance or spirit from a patient aided by that patient's belief in the magic used. With the afflicting substance removed, good health returned. The shamanic performance took place at night, in the home of the patient, beside a fire with many onlookers who joined with the shaman's singing/chanting. One healing rite is described:

"... **drumming** on a long plank was done by ten men hired for the purpose. The shaman, like a chief, had a **spokesman [talker]**, who repeated aloud what the spirit communicated to the shaman. . . .

All pre-adolescent children were sent away, especially babies. There was the danger that the "disease" taken from the patient's body might lodge in theirs; older people were not so susceptible. . . . There was a regular **costume** for practitioners [the shaman], which consisted essentially of a cap bearing eagle feathers [or, better, the emblem of that animal from which his *tahmahnawis* had been derived]. In addition, the shaman painted his face in various colors, wore buckskin leggings and shirt,. . . . Shamans had rattles made of a bunch of [deer?] dew-claws strung together. . . . A shaman always smoked before starting to cure, taking five puffs of his pipe and inhaling the smoke. This made his cure more effective since it made his spirit more active and strong.

A big fire was built beside which the patient was laid. The shaman sang his spirit songs to the accompaniment of the din created by whacking at the plank-drum, warmed his hands repeatedly at the fire beside him, and placed them on the sick man's stomach. The spirit power in his hands drew the 'disease' toward them. Then he applied his mouth to the spot to suck it out. In this manner he drew out 'blood, bad stuff.' Having gotten it into his mouth, he spat it into a vessel of water 'to cool it.' It was then more easily handled. Ordinarily it remained invisible to the laity although other shamans could see it readily enough. He would sometimes show a little object as the offending substance."[9]

But a shaman's status was not secure. His spirit power was liable to be stolen by another shaman possessed of a more powerful *tahmahnawis*. Even more hazardous, upon failing to effect a cure, or suspect in the causing of a curse, a shaman might be killed by the grieving family members.

E. Intent of the Work

This work, then, shows the Yakima shaman at work. The introductory chapter, reprinted and annotated from Kuykendall's original, takes us back almost to the first days of the reservation when traditional shamans were numerous. Then, thanks to McWhorter's collecting efforts, accounts of the shaman are included from about the turn of the century. There is no other record that we know of giving such details about the shaman's activities.

Because of the integrity of the original collectors in recording their observations, I believe that the credibility of the narratives is high. Even though McWhorter worked during the early twentieth century when the several Native American cultures and languages on the Yakima Reservation, although still strong and vital, had been subject to irreversible change, cultural intermingling, and even decline for 50-75 years, he sought out people who remembered the old ways. Our aim is twofold—to allow a wide public audience to understand a fascinating side to Yakima Indian culture. Second, I want to make available these authentic observations and narratives so that students of Indian life can appreciate the past, including beliefs and practices of this particular tribe, and marvel at the culture of this proud Indian nation.

F. Organization of the Work

The narrative texts given here were extracted from The Papers of Lucullus Virgil McWhorter, Washington State University Libraries, as cited in Nelson A. Ault 1959. *The Papers of Lucullus Virgil McWhorter*. Pullman: Friends of the Library, State College of Washington.

> Folder 1514: pp. 12, 16, 18, 44-47, 53-54, 58-114, 126-127
>
> Folder 1515: pp. 26-49, 50-60
>
> Folder 1516: pp. 20-24, 123-124
>
> Folder 1521: pp. 14
>
> Folder 1523: pp. 6
>
> Folder 1526: pp. 1-28, 51-54
>
> Folder 1527: pp. 7-8, 17-28, 33-53
>
> Folder 1528: p. 41

Folder 1531: pp. 3-5

Folder 1532: pp. 36-58

Folder 1539: pp. 55-65

Folder 1547: pp. 167-181

Folder 1614: pp. 24-29

Also, from The Papers of George Benson Kuykendall I have taken the draft version of "An Early Introduction to the Shaman and forms of Magic Among the Yakima Indians," the Carol Thompson transcription, 1973: "Indian Customs;" "Indian Traditions, Legends, Superstitions and customs;" and "Indian Customs and Traditions." 75 pp. See Hines, Donald M. 1976. *An Index of Archived Resources for a Folklife and Cultural History of the Inland Pacific Northwest Frontier*, p. 51. Ann Arbor: University Microfilms International.

Using photocopies of McWhorter's original texts supplied by the W.S.U. library staff, I have made only those minimal changes of spelling, direct discourse, or paragraphing to maximize reader understanding. The narratives have not been rewritten, but preserve the original sense of being told to McWhorter. I have followed McWhorter's lead and included Yakima words for the animals, places, phenomena. These terms are all-valuable in preserving a sense of milieu for the reader who is now far removed from the original setting and tribal milieu. To regularize McWhorter's spelling of the Yakima terms, (I believe he chose spelling that is a phonetic approximation of the oral language), I have consulted the word list which I compiled for *Ghost Voices. . .*, pp. 415-422. Most important, McWhorter's follow-up questioning and discussion with an informant on details about the shaman or shamanic experience have been carefully retained, for they underscore how central to Yakima life the shaman formerly was.

I have arranged the narratives into related categories for ease of reading, and to increase the reader's understanding of patterns of shamanic behavior.

I. AN EARLY INTRODUCTION TO THE SHAMAN AND FORMS OF MAGIC AMONG THE YAKIMA INDIANS.

Originally published by George B. Kuykendall, physician to the Yakima Indian Agency, this chapter reflects ten years' observation and note-taking. As such, it provides perhaps the earliest introduction from an interested observer to the Yakima shaman, his Acquisition of Spirit Power, Treatment of the Sick, Spiritualism as practiced by some shamans, Mourning Customs, Burial Customs, Rehabiliment [reclothing] of the Dead, and The Indians' Idea of the Soul and a Future State.

II. THE ORIGINS OF SHAMANS' POWER OR *TAHMAHNAWIS*.

Accounts in which shamans or others detail how they acquired their spirit power. Because of the Indians' strong belief in the supernatural, their youthful quest of spirit power or *tahmahnawis* into the dark night of a remote wilderness setting must have been fraught with absolute terror, as they thought of the ghosts, and the wild animals lurking in the darkness. Also, some *tahmahnawis* which a youth might acquire were bad. The unfortunate shaman possessing a bad *tahmahnawis* could do nothing to control it, might be killed or forced to flee the tribe for several years.

III. ACCOUNTS BY SHAMANS DESCRIBE THEIR HEALING POWERS WITH CORROBORATIVE STATEMENTS BY SEVERAL PATIENTS.

The Shaman *Nah-schoot* describes the origin of his healing powers, and relates several visions. Several patients relate of *Nah-schoot's* marvelous power that cured them of alcoholism and other afflictions. At least two accounts relate of the Yakima sorcerer, that feared spirit-worker who is possessed of an evil *tah*, and his acts.

IV. THE RATTLESNAKE AS SHAMAN'S SIMPLE.

Although birds, mammals and the physical landscape might give a youth *tahmahnawis*, the rattlesnake was an especially dreadful source of power. With the *tah* power of the rattlesnake, an Indian could understand their language, was able to discover their presence when the serpents were out of sight, and, most of all, was not affected by their venom. The shaman could handle the angry serpent and heal victims of snakebite.

V. REMARKABLE ACCOUNTS OF SHAMANS' *TAHMAHNAWIS* POWERS.

Numerous accounts describe the particular animal or object from which their *tahmahnawis* power was derived. **Aquatic** *tahs*, **protective** *tahs*, **premonitional** *tahs*, **protective dreams**, **malevolent** *tahs* **of the Yakima sorcerer**—tribesmen related these freely to

McWhorter.

VI. SOME MID-COLUMBIA TRIBAL TALES RECOUNTING THE DEATH JOURNEY VISION.

Related here are twelve accounts by Indians who died following a grievous accident or grave illness. They departed this world and began a trek to another place. But they are blocked, forced to return to earth to make atonement for evil deeds done in life. Then, reviving, even after several days time, the recently dead instructs those about him /her on living a good life, even identifying some who will follow next in death.

In this collection each narrative bears a title given originally by the Indian source or by the collector. Then, each narrative is assigned a number which marks its place within the volume. Where possible the informant is named and the time given when the narrative was taken down.

To assist the reader, several informational features are appended hereafter. First, an **Index of Motifs** lists traditional details of character, plot or other background details in the Death Vision Journey narratives. Second, **Notes to the Narratives** provide explanatory details about the narratives, taken from informants to McWhorter, or supplied by this writer and so marked "DH". Third, a **Selected List of Readings** of useful works on the shaman and his labors is included. Finally, **Acknowledgements** of sources and individuals to whom I am indebted concludes this work.

PART TWO

CHAPTER ONE

AN EARLY INTRODUCTION TO THE SHAMAN AND FORMS OF MAGIC AMONG THE YAKIMA INDIANS[10],[11],[12]

INTRODUCTION

Dr. George [Benson] Kuykendall was Yakima Agency physician at Fort Simcoe, Washington Territory, from 1872 to 1882. A recent graduate of medical school, in debt and in poor health, he accepted the post of physician to the tribes and bands of the Yakima Indian Reservation. He notes, "I arrived with my family at Fort Simcoe in July, 1872, and entered upon one of the most interesting periods of my life, a period marked by experiences not common to the average medical man. Some of these experiences were thrilling—all were interesting. Here at the Fort I had the medical oversight of a large corps of government employees and instructors, pupils of the Indian schools, and about sixteen hundred Indians. Besides, there was an extensive range of practice among the outside settlements. The white people at the Fort had a two-fold mission; first, as government employes [sic.], secondly, as missionaries, whose object was to instruct the Indians in the white man's ways and civilization. A complete history of events and our experiences while there would make an interesting volume.

"Soon after arriving at Fort Simcoe, Major Powell, of the Department of Ethnology in the Smithsonian Institution, at Washington, D.C., wrote me asking me to take up in behalf of the government, the study of Indian ethnology, language, folk lore; their myths, traditions and beliefs and their ancient customs and usages. This, being undertaken, made a sort of diversion from the regular routine of my medical duties. A large amount of data was accumulated, and later, part of it was printed and published, and has since gone into and become a part of the history of the state of Washington."[13] Upon leaving service with the Yakima Agency, Kuykendall continued to practice medicine in Pomeroy, Washington, for many years. At his death, his papers were placed in the Washington State University Library, Pullman, Washington.

Annotative notes to Kuykendall's observations hereafter derive from Murdock, G.P. 1965. "Tenino Shamanism," *Ethnology* 4:165-171 [hereafter cited as "Murdock: page"]. Also, Spier, Leslie and Edward Sapir 1930. *Wishram Ethnography*, UWPA 3/3. Seattle: University of Washington Press, esp. pp. 236-248 [hereafter cited as "Spier, Wishram: page"]. My annotation of Kuykendall's observations serves several purposes. First, relating Kuykendall's findings against reports of the shaman from nearby tribes attests to the reliability of his observations. Second, by relating similarities or differences of shamans and their magic from nearby tribes, I hope the nature of shamanistic endeavor will be made clearer to the reader. Finally, this volume sets forth basic accounts of shamanic activities as narrated by shamans or their patients or close friends from among the Yakimas and elsewhere— and Kuykendall's chapter provides an invaluable context.

But Kuykendall's observations grate on modern sensibilities, for he was a skeptic (the result of his medical training), and he held strong opinions reflective of the officials and the functions of the Indian Agency at Fort Simcoe. His Son, Elgin V. Kuykendall, recalls, "Father had considerable difficulty persuading the Indians to discard the incantations of the Indian medicine men and submit to proper medical treatment. They had been taught for generations to believe that illness was the work of some evil spirit, which had to be driven out of the body by some sort of magic or sorcery, and was never ascribed to disfunction of the organs of the body."[14]

E. V. Kuykendall recalled that on one occasion, with his son in tow, G.B. Kuykendall drove several miles from Fort Simcoe to treat a young Indian man ill of an evil spirit—but who was physically sound. The youth ". . . finally admitted that a certain medicine man had communicated "*mesatchee tamanawash*" [an evil spell?] to him and that he was doomed to die." But G.B. Kuykenkdall resorted to ". . . a little hocuspocus of his own invention." First, he told the youth that he (GBK) had a stronger power than the medicine man. Second, he promised to drive the spirit out of the youth. Third, that when Kuykendall told the youth to arise, he was to mount his horse, take a brisk ride. Thus, the spirit would be gone.[15] Kuykendall ". . . made a few magic passes over the boy, muttered a few phony incantations over him, and not only told him to get up but jerked him to his feet, pushed him out of the house toward his horse and ordered him to mount the animal and ride away. He was soon hidden by a cloud of dust as his horse sped away through the sand and sage."[16]

We do an immense disservice by judging Kuykendall in terms of our present standards for accepting diversity, but also by our accumulated body of knowledge. First, Kuykendall was trained as a physician, and his scientific training led him to scorn Indian shamanism. But there were other causes for his bias. A religious context shaped Kuykendall's outlook, for "Father Wilbur," the Rev. James Harvey Wilbur, was not only Yakima Indian Agent, but also Methodist cleric to the Indians. The mission of the Agency was to "instruct the Indians in the white man's ways and civilization," and Kuykendall also served as Sunday School Superintendent. Third, in his response to Native Americans Kuykendall probably reflects the historical milieu about him. But if Kuykendall failed to understand the psychology witting/unwittingly employed by the shaman,[17] we should remember that during his time among the Indians—in distant New York the foundations for psychology were only then being laid—by William James, *The Principles of Psychology* (1890), and others.

These are George B. Kuykendall's observations and interpretations:

TAMANOWASH OR SPIRIT POWER[18]

Among the Indians of the Northwest, religion,

sorcery and medicine were all mixed up together. The term "doctor" is a misnomer for the Indian medicine man. Shaman, conjuror or witch would come nearer expressing the truth. The Indian idea of disease was not that it is caused by anything wrong in the workings of the physical organism, but by some unseen power or spirit which they call "*tamanowash.*"[19] They acknowledged the existence of disease as we understand it when the disease is visible and causes changes of structure, such as boils, skin diseases, cuts, wounds of all kinds and scrofulous [?] ulcers, etc. These were accepted as being under dominion of ordinary medicine. Usually, such cases are considered amenable to material remedies, that may be taken internally or applied externally. But, if any disease or ailment whatever terminated fatally, then *tamanowash* had something to do with it. When asked what "*tamanowash*" is, an Indian never can tell except by way of giving illustrative cases of the supposed *tamanowash* power. It is nothing more than a form of witchcraft.[20]

The "doctor" or medicine man's power to cure or kill comes from collusion or compact in a peculiar manner with the spirits of the dead, or of living animals, or dead men, or of lakes, mountains, rivers, springs, fountains, trees, stones, or any inanimate object.[21,22] The old Indian idea is that in everything there is a kind of vital essence or force independent of the material thing itself. This force or influence may be communicated to a man, may reside in him or be subject to his bidding, or the man may be ruled or dominated by the influence or spirit (K, p. 6). Either sex may have the *tamanowash* power.[23,24] Those who become doctors or get the "big-medicine power" always get it in a mysterious, supernatural way. *Tamanowash* is the general term for the invisible witch [magic?] power (K, p.6). "*Tah*" is the special manifestation of *tamanowash* in some particular form or shape. The Indians say that those who become medicine men have the fact revealed to them while young. Boys who have never "known women," or girls who have not "known men," are the terms they use in describing the age. The great medicine power never comes to those who have been contaminated by the opposite sex.

The *tamanowash*-doctor power is nearly always communicated in the night-time. At about age seven to eleven or twelve years of age is considered the most likely time a boy or girl will "see *tah*" or "get *tah*."[25],[26] A boy or girl of the proper age went out alone to some strange place at night time and might see a coyote, badger, bat, or even a moth; and he or she will hear a voice speaking. The coyote will howl, or the owl may screech or hoot, but in some strange, mysterious manner it conveys to the excited youth intelligible ideas, the message he is expecting, which may be in the form of a command to do something.[27],[28] Whatever the words spoken may be, they are to be remembered. If then nothing is said [about the *tah* incident] until the youth comes to adult age,[29],[30],[31] then he will be a doctor, and the communication he received must be sung as a *tamanowash* song at the incantations of that doctor over the sick.[32] A real doctor can tell when a child has had "*tah*" communicated to him, but other people cannot (K:6-7).[33]

If this communication be remembered until

the candidate reaches maturity, he will be a medicine man. Sometimes the *tamanowash* power is communicated in a more terrible and impressive manner. The person is met in some dark, lonely place by a fiery, shining animal, or a walking human skeleton of huge proportions illuminated within by a mysterious light. The eye sockets of this strange being gleam and flash like burning fire. Within the chest between the ribs is seen a great heart swinging and beating from side to side; while thunders roll and lightnings flash in the face of the terrified beholder, who falls to the earth unconscious. While he remains in a trance-like condition, the wonderful apparition speaks to him in a dream, telling him what to do. He is commissioned to heal, destroy or prophesy. When he comes out of his trance, the strange being is gone; and he is alone in silence and darkness. He is now a doctor and has *tamanowash* power, and never during life can he get rid of it. If any one's *tah* leaves him or is taken away by some stronger doctor, then that one [the first doctor] will die. One doctor may receive *tah* from a great many different objects or animals, and will be of course so much the "stronger doctor"(K:78).[34] In many of the tribes the candidate, before entering upon his business, went off into some lonely mountain cave or unfrequented place and then fasted until lank and haggard, and filled with superstitious frenzy. He then came from his place of retirement emaciated and with glittering, diabolic eyes, wild with excitement, hideously painted and almost naked. Raving and yelling like a maniac, he rushed among his friends. Seizing the flesh of their arms in his teeth, he bit out a mouthful and devoured it like a ravening beast. Strange to say, among some tribes it was considered a matter of honor to be able to show the scars made by these frantic human devils.[35]

Among some tribes north of Puget Sound in British Columbia, these shamans or conjurors actually ate human dead bodies, or attacked and devoured dogs. The Clallams and Nisquallies came nearer following the practices of the Indians farther north in these respects. A young person who has received *tah* spirit or influence must not try to exercise his powers until adult age. About 40 is as early an age as the men began to doctor; women doctored younger. According to this arrangement all one has to do to be a doctor is to claim to have received the spirit of *tamanowash* while young, and to go on and operate. If he succeeds at the outset, then he is in fair way to be recognized soon as a strong *"tawati"* or *tamanowash* man (K:8). The Columbia River Indians: Klikitats, Okanagan, and others used to send their children at night to the "houses of the dead" to listen to what the dead might say. In some instances they whipped their children and drove them out for this purpose.(K:8)[36],[37] If a man had a son whom he wished to grow up a doctor, he would send him to some lonely place with instructions to look out for *"tah."* Filled with horrid fears, and with an excited imagination, the young fellow would hear or imagine he heard a voice from some object, animate or inanimate; and he gets credentials before long, and with little cost except the shock to his nervous system.[38] Those who went often and never received a call from *tah* were considered to be for some cause unfitted for the mysteries and dignities of the "big medicine," the doctor's office. The Indian idea is that some spirit speaks through an animal, bird or thing which communicates the *tamanowash* power. The kind of animal or object from which the *tamanowash* is received indicates to some extent the scope or power of the doctor.[39] For instance, a man inspired by the rattlesnake is a "snake doctor," can handle rattlesnakes without danger, and can cure snake bites. Should a snake bite him, he would not die. A doctor receiving his *tamanowash* from the *tlchachie* (ghosts)[40] can handle corpses or go into the "dead-houses" or graves, and can communicate with the dead; and the spirits of the dead will hold converse with him; all of which things are impossible to ordinary persons. Some "medicine men" can bring the Chinook wind; some can bring rain by virtue of having a thunder *tah* or spirit (K:8-9). Others cause the salmon to come up the river; and others still can influence the huckleberry crops. A very "strong doctor" may have a variety of powers, and be capable of doing many wonderful things.[41] Some have claimed to be able to eat fire, drink boiling water, or wash in scalding water because they had the "fire spirit." Any real *tawati* could cause a person to sicken and die. The death might be sudden or lingering on from month to month or for years even, as in consumption or other wasting diseases(K:9).[42]

Indian doctors often admitted they had killed certain persons and threatened to kill others.[43] Threats of this kind were made to extort favors or frighten others into doing what the "medicine man" desired done. Not very infrequently marriages were broken up and business transactions stopped by threats of the medicine man (K:9). In some few cases it was said the medicine man could not help killing or causing others to sicken.

The *tamanowash* overpowered him and dominated his actions against his will. The *tamanowash* was offended; and the life of the victim was the penalty, the doctor being the unfortunate medium of this direful calamity. Usually the *tawati* was held to be fully accountable and even charged with the most extravagant absurdities.[44] However, the populace was careful not to offend the doctors (K:10).

Sickness caused by the doctors was called "*tamanowash* sick;" and no material medicine could ever have any influence in curing ailments of this class.[45] The way the *tamanowash* man bewitches or "gives *tamanowash*" to another is generally by looking or gazing upon the person. In many instances, however, the doctors are accused of causing sickness when the individual has not been seen by them for a long time. A common expression among the Indians to denote the bewitching or *tamanowashing* of a person is to say: "he has been shot" by the doctor (K:10).[46] The evil spirit must be exorcised or killed or "pulled out."[47] The disease is considered to be a living entity that has entered the person; and often the old *tamanowash* man makes a diagnosis of a "bug in the stomach or heart:" or a "worm or worms in the heart" or limbs. These astute doctors or conjurors even go on to give the size of the insect or animal, tell its color and describe its malevolent antics in the system. The superstitious bystanders, with protuberant eyes and mouths agape, swallow the whole thing as fact indisputable. Frequently the person sick claims to have no pain anywhere; there is no fever, no observable disorder of any of the functions. He is sick though—he knows he has *tamanowash* sickness because he had some new or uncommon sensation or feeling while passing a doctor or when some doctor looked at him, or because some doctor was offended at him and threatened him. In such a case the Indians say no physical remedy can do any good. If a physician visits such a person and gives medicine and the patient recovers, then it was not a real case of *tamanowash* sickness, or if (which is common) the Indians have had one of their own doctors to see the case, the [latter] Indian doctor gets the credit for the cure. This is invariably the case unless they conclude possibly it was not "Indian sickness." They are in the habit of calling the *tamanowash* trouble "Indian sickness" because it is peculiar to themselves (K:11). But the patient feels that the *tamanowash* has entered him, and that he is going to die. He has the "Indian sickness," *tamanowash* sickness—in short, is bewitched. In such a case, it is the spirit or soul that is sick. We would say it was a case of imagination. There must be a big *pow-wow* to exorcise the demoniac influence.

The medicine man cannot exercise his *tamanowash* powers over a white person, though they can bewitch a half breed if the half-breed has the "Indian heart." If he has the "white man's heart," then the doctor's *tamanowash* will not affect him (K:11); which is equal to saying that the Indian doctor can influence anyone who is superstitious and credulous enough to imagine he has this wonderful *tamanowash* power. The emanation from the doctors which kills or cures is called, by most of the tribes of the Northwest, *towtenook*, or "medicine." This *towtenook* has no special properties of healing. It is a sort of [magical?] power working according to the will of the person from whom it may emanate; and the same *towtenook* may kill or cure as the shaman wills it to do. The Indians had really very little knowledge of the effects of diseases on the internal organism. They believed recovery would surely follow if only the offending *tamanowash* could be expelled, or as the Indians say, "pulled out," "drawn out," "put away," or "killed."[48] The wasted form of the consumptive, or the poisoned blood and exhausted vitality of the typhoid-fever patient formed no bar to recovery, provided the bad medicine was eliminated someway.

In case of the death of a patient, the attending doctor or doctors invariably say some other doctors have killed the patient. Sometimes they admit the opposing *tamanowash* was too strong, and they could not displace it or "pull it out."[49] If some other doctor has attended the patient, before the last one charges the death to the first one; the patient, often before death, charges his death equally upon all who have attended him.[50] Often again, all the doctors combine to say that some other strange *tawati* has done the mischief, and often they name the particular one. The grand object of course is to shift the responsibility from self to someone else. It is common to employ a number of doctors, thinking that their combined power may be able to "pull out" the offending *towtenook* or *tamanowash*(K:11).[51,52] In event of death of a patient, the doctor always attempted to screen himself by charging the death upon some other doctor. This was the only occasion when the medicine man was willing to acknowledge any other doctor was stronger; and it was then a matter of self-protection. If some other doctor had been conjuring about the patient, and had made a failure to cure, the next doctor called would likely as not say the first one was causing the sickness; and a good deal of [interpersonal] friction would ensue.

The Indians believe there are some doctors who never make themselves known—these are always the "bad kind." It used to be not uncommon for someone to be accused of doctoring or making people sick who made no pretense of being a doctor; much the same as some persons were formerly accused of being witches among the whites. To persistently deny the charge had not the least effect to change the opinion of the people if once the name of doctor became fastened to a person by current rumor. Doctors from a distance are much sought. There is a sort of belief that strange medicine men from some other place than the immediate vicinity of the sick generally are more successful (K:12).

It was firmly believed that just before death the dying person would have it revealed to him who the offending *tamanowash* man was that was causing the sickness and death.[53] Such a statement was implicitly believed, and was regarded something as "dying statements" have been by civilized courts, that is, received without oath or questioning. In prolonged cases, frequently several conjurors were called; and they usually managed to agree upon throwing the blame on some distant doctor; which poor medico, being out of seeing or hearing distance, the load of the great crime was not very afflicting; and this very convenient arrangement enabled the medical conclave to get off with the honors and emoluments of the occasion, and escape the responsibility for a failure. If the patient died, however, no matter what the disease or condition, the verdict of the friends was "*wake skookum tocta*;" which classical Chinook almost any old pioneer would understand to be equivalent to saying that the doctors for the occasion were rather small fry. As in the days of witchcraft, so among the Indians; persons who disavowed all claim of being "doctor" were accused of giving *tamanowash* or bewitching people. Unfortunately, the accused had no power to prove their innocence, as protestations on their part were of no avail. Such persons were in a bad predicament. The Indians believed that, as they had caused the sickness, they could cure it; and they were urged to do so, and even threatened. If to save themselves they yielded and engaged in *pow-wowing*, then of course the name of being doctor was fixed irrevocably. The glory of the "medicine man" was far from being unalloyed; and he always stood a chance of getting a speedy passport to the country where there was no field for the exercise of his powers.

The doctor among the Indians is much more dreaded than loved. If he is treated respectfully, it is because of fear of his dreaded power—while they thus fear him and often hate him and speak of him as a rattlesnake or wolf, they are sure to send for him in sickness. Many employ the doctors in cases where they would not but for fear of offending them and incurring their displeasure. In assemblies and councils the doctors are shied away from, and they have in numerous instances been charged with sitting near the doorways and "shooting with *tamanowash*" those who came in.[54] Children are taught to fear the doctors, so that they dread to meet them and will shy away and keep out of sight when the *tawatie* comes along (K:12).[55]

There were many kinds of doctors.[56] Some profess to cure snake bites and some spider bites, etc. (K:12). Some operated in one specialty only, while the big doctors (*n-chee' twatima*)[57] profess to be equal to almost any emergency, and often were reported to have resuscitated dead persons. Among these conjurors were those who were not considered to have the "big medicine." There were some who were called half-doctors (*wootkt twati*) or small doctors (*ix-pix twati*). These all worked by sorcery; however, they are not often accused of killing anyone. These, I should imagine, were rather the happier class as they get a fair share of glory and not much blame (K:13). The Klikitats and Yakimas called one class of these the "*pamiss-pamiss itta*" doctors, that is, those who have the power to charm or control the minds or feelings of others, but as applied to the doctor means more—has a more extended and variable meaning. While the *pamiss pamiss itta* has the ability to cast a spell or charm over the minds of others so as to soften anger, change purposes or will, or even compel a certain course of action (K:13). These were often old women or old men,[58] who generally exercised their peculiar functions in a different and less ostentatious manner. Their power was invoked to charm away the spirits that linger about and poison the food of those in mourning, or who have committed murder, during his days of his purification. They of this class tell the fortunes of war and of the chase, whisper over the sick, or those fallen into a sudden fit to divine whether such are to recover. No one can understand anything the *pamiss pamiss itta*[59] say, even when they speak out loudly in their sorceries. The Indians say that *pamiss pamiss ittama* of the same spirit or *tah* can understand each other. The whole thing is a base fraud, of course, but strangely enough the Indians swallow it all as verity itself. Lying down upon the earth listening and whispering unintelligible gibberish, they claimed to divine what was going on in the distant chase or battle. They also mumbled over those fallen into a faint or fit to divine whether the sickness would be fatal, and to otherwise exercise a benign influence upon the sufferer.

There are also the "baby understanders" and the "dog understanders," two other functionaries that pass under the name of "*ix-six tawatis*," or "little doctors." The "baby understander" or, as they say the *meanus ashuquat*, professes to be able to understand all the thoughts and feelings of a baby. What a fine thing it would be for white physicians to have one of these wise ones at hand when attending infants! This *meanus ashuquat* ought certainly to have all the dignity and honor of a true *tawati* instead of being called a "small doctor:" or "half doctor"(K:14)!

There is a common belief among all the Pacific Northwest Indians that dogs and little infants could communicate together.[60] The dog understands the baby and the baby understands the dog. Nearly invariably, when the child grows up and learns to speak Indian, he then forgets the dog language. Now and then one man or woman retains this wonderful gift, and then he or she becomes a kind of interpreter to let the friends know what is troubling the child in case of sickness (K:14). This may partly explain the great love the Indian has for his dogs; for it is a fact that often the Indian would consider the striking or kicking of his dog to be a worse insult than to be struck himself. There are certain "small doctors" who claim to be "baby understanders" and "dog understanders;" and, strange to say, the services of these functionaries are or were not infrequently brought into requisition. How these dog and baby linguists acquire the faculty of interpreting canine and infant whinings is variously explained; but there is always mystery about it. Sometimes it is through inspiration by the dog spirit; or, once in a while, a talented baby fails to forget the dog language at the time he acquires the Indian tongue; and of course he would be a suitable person for interpreter to unfold dog and baby lore. Though white people do not know it, the whinings of dogs, and the infant "da, da" babbling, all mean something—are attempts to make known their wants. These dog or baby understanders can interpret all this for the enlightenment and edification of Indian humanity.

A common notion among these tribes is that a baby sickens or dies of its own accord, or because something has been done or said that is displeasing to it. Under these circumstances the wonderful dog or baby "understander" has an opportunity to show his skill. If a child cries or frets and is cross, and jabbers and mumbles a great deal and seems to be about half sick, as babies often do, the Indian people imagine the baby is trying to say something; and that, especially if it jabbers and makes such sounds as children from six to twelve months old usually do; and that, unless its language is interpreted, it will die. When these pretentious interpreters [*meranus ashuquat*] undertake a case, the baby is taken into their arms; and some kind of medicine song is sung, the body being swayed backward and forward; and the little one is asked such questions as "What troubles you?" "Have you not been fed enough?" "Have they not given you warm clothes?" "Has any one spoken lightly or derisively of you?" "Does anyone want you to die so as to get the property you would inherit?" "Do you not like your parents and friends?" "Do you want to go to the spirit land to your brothers and sisters?" "Are the spirits trying to get you away from us?" etc. After various performances, the "doctor," he or she, then professes to get an answer and then sings again when the friends have promised to rectify matters. If the friends get an idea that a child is sick on account of something of this kind, they say it will never recover until the "baby understander" comes and interprets its communications and tries to mollify its feelings (K:15). Whatever was troubling the baby must be removed and its wishes obeyed; and it would recover—otherwise, it would die.

It was commonly believed that a "dog understander" [*koosi koosi ashuquat*] holds communication with a dog, and the dog relates things that have transpired in the absence of its master or mistress. To illustrate this Indian idea or notion, I give the following which was related to me by a halfbreed young woman who speaks good English. At the Cascades [tribe] on the Columbia River there lived a few years ago one of these "dog understanders"—an old woman. She lived near this halfbreed woman's mother's place and was very poor and daily went away to gather berries or roots for subsistence, leaving her little dog to watch her lodge. The halfbreed woman had often noticed the old squaw talking to her dog. One evening when the old woman came in from her day's rambles, her dog met her and jumped about wagging his tail, and gave evidence of being much pleased at his mistress' return. While he was whining and frisking about, the old woman said, "Well, they are rich, and we are poor," to the dog.

The halfbreed girl said to her mother, "Why does the old woman talk to her dog so?"

"Her mother informed her that the old woman professed to understand the dog, and said the dog talked to her. They concluded to list [test?] the matter, and the next day when the old woman went away, they opened the door of her lodge and went in, the little dog following.

They said, "Now we will see if the dog will tell the old woman about it."

In the evening the old woman came back, and her dog ran out to meet her as usual. She said to the halfbreed girl and her mother, "My dog says you were in my house while I was gone."

They still did not credit the old woman's story of understanding the dog. And next day when she was gone, they went into her lodge and turned things over, and rolled them about, but put them back the same before. The little dog [was] standing by all the time.

In the evening when the old woman returned she said, "My dog tells me you were in my house and stole something. She was then informed that they had been trying to test whether her dog did talk or not, and had been in and turned things about, but had not taken anything; but now they believed she really understood the dog, and the dog understood her. Of course the whole thing does not amount to a row of pins for probably the old woman was suspicious and had so arranged her door or marked things that any move would immediately be detected. Such things, however, are swallowed as demonstrated truth by the Indians (K:16-17).

TREATMENT OF THE SICK

The treatment of the sick among the Indians was and is only a sort of conjuring. The *"tawatis"* or "big medicines" use no material remedies whatever. Indian doctoring or treatment of the sick is really only a contest between contending doctors or *tamanowash* spirits. When a person is sick, it is because some doctor has given that individual *tamanowash*, and the question is who is strong enough a doctor to overcome the offending doctor's *tah* or *tamanowash* power (K:17). Among some of the tribes in Southern Oregon the shaman used to cut a small bit of buckskin, and slit the skin of the body and work the bit gradually under. This was done under cover of blankets or skins, so that the operator's hands were out of sight of patient and surrounding spectators. This bit of buckskin was charmed or had some mysterious magic power of sinking down into the body and destroying the disease.

Each doctor has his friends and patrons who trust him and employ him and do not believe he causes others to be sick. More frequently, each gen [=clan] has its own doctor or doctors for ordinary cases (K:17). When in case of sickness the medicine man is sent for, the price is agreed upon beforehand;[61] and in nearly all cases a cure is promised before the patient is seen. The common idea among the Indians is no cure—no pay;[62] but the doctor always gets the pay or nearly always whether recovery or death ensues (K:17). Often the doctor announces the diagnosis before going to the patient. Of course he could cure anything; otherwise why should he be a big-medicine man at all; and, besides, an expression of distrust as to his ability would brand him with the name of being no good. The Indian wants a sure thing or nothing; and, though the theory is no cure no pay, the doctor generally was smart enough to get his pay, kill or cure. The expectation is that recovery is to be speedy. I [Kuykendall] have known doctoring to be kept up for two or three weeks and, often, for several days at intervals for a long time (K:17-18). The doctor has been known to promise perfect recovery in one day of a patient far gone in consumption, and who had not a ghost of a chance of ever being any better.

The medicine man, when called, is supposed to wear his official hat, his *tamanowash* hat or doctor's hat. He may always be known by this.[63] There is no definite form or style for this, but it is usually different from that worn by others. If the doctor professes to have the "bear *tamanowash*," he wears a bearskin hat—maybe the skin of a bear's head with ears on and with bear's claws and teeth fastened on to it. If he has Owl *tah* or *tamanowash*, then he may have an owlskin cap and plume of owl feathers, etc. (K:18). His official badge may be from the owl, beaver, or any animal or thing by virtue of whose spirit he performs his exorcisms.[64] The terms for the cure being settled, the conjuror sets out to see his patient, and enters the lodge invested with all the dignity and solemnity, and mystery as well, that he can bring to the occasion. His movements are all very deliberate, as should be the case on momentous occasions. Going in, he seats himself by the side of the patient.[65] He is not expected to ask the location of pain or discomfort; for, as a matter of course, he knows all about that better than the patient himself. He places his hands on the body, or upon any part of which the patient complains; presses down and retains his hands in position some time. Often, he heats them by the fire and replaces them,[66] and goes through various strokings or cabalistic maneuvers. After a time he probably announces his diagnosis to the gaping bystanders. He may announce where the *tamanowash* is in the body. Generally, it is said to be in the heart, no matter what the complaint is (K:18). With a solemn visage, he may state that the man has a spider in his heart. The spider spirit is big medicine. Some of the tribes say that the grand-sachem *tamanowash* is in the shape of a giant spider. The doctor not only tells what the animal is, but gives the size, color, shape, and everything in such a circumstantial manner that the common Indians believe it. How could he describe it so minutely if he did not see it? He is careful to explain that he can extract the insect *secundum artem tamanowashem*. In many instances a fly or maggot is said to be the cause of the sickness, particularly if there be some kind of ulcer. Whatever the medicine man may diagnosticate, the patient has *tamanowash* sickness; and generally it is caused by some evil-disposed doctor; and nothing will work a cure but to "make medicine" or go through their *pow-wows* and conjuring.[67,68]

The night time is usually selected for the

healing ceremony, though they doctor any time. The Indian doctor always sings or goes through an incantation and then asks all who are present [in the lodge or winter longhouse] to assist him. The assistants are expected to drum; with short clubs or sticks from sixteen inches to two feet long upon some boards or poles which are laid along in front of the performers. Frequently, there are two rows of drummers, one on the left and the other on the right of the lodge, with the patient between and the shaman sits near him. The position of the parties is not essential. The doctor is master of ceremonies[69] and directs as to the drumming. No matter how sick the patient may be, the noise must go on. The Indians say the drumming is to help the doctor and to assist in driving away the *tamanowash* from the sick person (K:18-19). The medicine man begins his incantations, and all join in. He generally sits cross-legged, "tailor fashion," and sways his body backward and forward; and, with his arms bent at right angles, he swings them backward and forward or in and out. With their clattering, drumming and lugubrious singing, they make about as ear-splitting and hideous a medley of sounds as could be imagined.[70] After the doctor and all get pretty well warmed up, he will urge them to drum more vigorously telling them that he is about ready to draw out the sickness.[71] Sometimes he may keep the drumming going a long time. Just before he goes through the performance of "drawing out" the *tamanowash*, he invokes the aid of the [his] spirit by which he exorcises the disease, and then he gets down over the patient and goes through motions as if he were pulling something out of the chest or stomach; sometimes the mouth is applied and the *tamanowash* sucked out. The doctor will announce that he now has the *tamanowash* and calls for a knife to cut it in two. Sometimes he cuts it all up and blows it away.[72] In some instances the *tamanowash*, when it comes out of the sick person, enters into the doctor, and he may dance about like a demon or someone crazy and fall down as if dead or insensible. In other cases he will lie and groan so as to be heard a great way off (K: 19).

The medicine man often takes a mouthful of water and blows it in a fine spray over the patient's body, and often in his excitement becomes violent, kneading or thumping the victim's body. He often grasps the flesh of the chest or abdomen in his ample mouth, and begins sucking to draw out the offending disease, or probably to impress the mind of the sick man and his friends. A common occurrence towards the close, when the excitement has got wrought up to a high pitch, is for the conjuror to go through motions of extracting something from the patient's body, twisting, grunting and sweating, as if the effort were tremendous. Then, he pretends he has the thing or animal in his hands, and perhaps takes a butcher knife and goes through the motions of hacking it into bits, and then, holding it up, blows it away. A sigh of relief escapes from the friends; the doctor has the demon devil or whatever it is by the heels or by some other secure grasp, and the patient is saved. The Indians look on this with profound awe, if not admiration; the doctor is a genius, a conjuror of spirits, a worker of wonders!

In one instance which I know, occurring during the winter 1881, the doctor had been doctoring a girl sick with consumption at intervals for months. She was growing worse and worse. He had been promising that she would be up and well again in a few days for a long time. Seeing she was failing fast, the friends kept urging him to do something immediately and to remove the *tamanowash*. One evening when the house was full, he said he would finish the work and "pull out" the *tamanowash* once for all. He told the friends that when the evil spirit came out it would probably strongly affect him, and they would have to take hold of him, for he would be crazy and might rush out of the house and run away. Finally, after singing for some time, the friends were directed to stand by, ready to hold him. "Now! Now!" said he. "Now I have it; hold me!" And he began to jump and rave like a maniac.[73] Several strong men got hold of him and put cords around him to prevent his doing something desperate. The girl died two days afterward, and the doctor was murdered in consequence (K:19-20).[74]

If, however, the patient should die next day or soon, they would want to knock him [the shaman] on the head with a hatchet. Thus fickle is fame;—the man who is a hero and demigod today may be a slaughtered devil tomorrow. The ceremony is not always the same. It varies a great deal in different tribes; but the drumming and hideous "singing" have been everywhere practiced. No matter what the state of the patient's nervous system, or how low in disease, the head-splitting plutonian racket must go on. Many a poor soul has been thumped and drummed out of time into eternity who perhaps if let alone would have recovered. The shaman often worked himself into almost a frenzy of excitement, so that he fell into a sort of cataleptic state, or had convulsions. The doctors say that in some instances the *tamanowash*, when exorcised and coming out of the patient, enters into the doctor like the devils of old went into the swine;[75] and he becomes crazy and raves around like a demon, and falls as if dead or insensible. In other cases he will groan as if about to die, so as to be heard a great way off. Of course, when he ceases groaning and gets up, he has triumphed over the *tamanowash* spirit and conquered the disease.

There are a few doctors who profess to have a mysterious patron spirit which they call *skaiap*.[76] The Indians say this spirit or influence always comes to the medicine man [*tawatis*] as a voice, and is never seen. It is the prince of all the spirits of evil. The commands of *skaiap* must be obeyed. This *skaiap tamanowash* causes insanity, and all forms of madness and epileptic fits. To disobey the voice of *skaiap* will bring death. It may be sudden, or lingering and painful. Numerous cases are told of where *skaiap* has caused people to become frenzied and wild (K: 20). Indians have no doubt become crazed through the belief that they were affected by this demoniac power. *Skaiap* sometimes commands the most painful and distressing things to be done. One was to swallow alive a great quantity of black water beetles, and another to sing *tamanowash* songs day and night for five years. In this case it was kept up for some time, about two years, and then relaxed; and, in consequence, the woman took sick, her knees were stiffened with the lower leg at right angles to the thigh, and she walked for a long time on her knees only, and finally died with a painful tumor of the breast because she had mortally offended this

mysterious *skaiap*. This occurred at the Cascades
[tribe] on the Columbia River. From the account given
me [Kuykendall], I presume the woman died of cancer
of the breast (K:21).

If a medicine man has the *skaiap tamanowash*,
and it leaves him or is driven out by some other
tamanowash man, then the [first] medicine man so
deserted will die—usually, they say, he becomes a
raving maniac and persists in jumping into the fire
until roasted to death. I [Kuykendall] have heard
intelligent Indians tell these things with an air of
perfect credulity. Indians who could speak English
well! The Indians say the whites are different from
them. They talk as if the Indian had within his body a
kind of life essence or spirit which may be taken away
for a time, and the person continue to live. But if it
does not soon return, then the person will die (K:21-
22).

The explanation of how a doctor takes away
the *tamanowash* from a person is something as follows
usually. If the man [doctor] has the horse's spirit for
his helper in curing or "working medicine," then the
tamanowash of the sick man is forced to mount the
horse spirit and is carried away, and then the man
[patient] will die unless it can be restored to him again.
One old Indian doctor has two *tahs* or spirits: one of
them Mount Adams, and the other of the elk. When
this old doctor wants to kill a person, he causes his elk
spirit to take the man's *tamanowash* and to run away
to the snow-clad mountain with it, and then the man
dies. Often, the doctors are accused of removing or
"taking away" this *tamanowash*; for this spirit or
essence, whatever it is, they call *tamanowash* also, but

it is not understood to be the doctor's kind of *tamanowash*. It is something possessed by all Indians, but not by the whites. This is a true picture, and shows how dark and dreadful was the cloud of superstition that darkened the lives of the aborigines of this country.

Besides the *tamanowash* doctors or conjurors, there was a class of medicos who administered remedies internally. Decoctions of herbs, roots and barks were given for fevers, colds, coughs and other ailments. These doctors were mostly women. The big-medicine power was mostly exercised by men. The two had a different name. Those who gave material remedies or *"pluh;"* were *"pluhitla;"* while the "big-medicine" power was exercised by the *"tawati."* These *"pluhitla"* often attempted to magnify their calling and increase their importance by creating as much mystery as possible about their business. It was a common notion among the Indians that bad blood or too much blood was the cause of much sickness. One of the offices of these "small doctors" was to bleed by opening a vein or by sucking the blood out through the skin. Frequently, the scalp was cut to allow blood to flow to relieve headache. In many diseases they believed there was blood collected at a part which caused pain or distress. The actual cauterizing or burning with a hot iron was a favorite remedy for rheumatism and stiffened joints. I [Kuykendall] have seen the scars from these procedures covering the joints and all along the spine. When an Indian takes medicine, he wants visible results, and the more sudden and violent the better. Medicines to produce vomiting were much sought; and power[ful?] purgatives were much thought of. Some of the doctors acquired considerable popularity on account of their skill in sucking blood from the bodies of patients. As this performance was a source of revenue, they of course managed to make business whenever they could; and they generally succeeded in discovering that there was too much blood or bad blood in every case, and that recovery could not possibly occur unless it was drawn out.

Some of these doctors practiced a good deal of chicanery in their manipulations. To equip themselves more fully for their sanguinary operations, and enable them to bring copious supplies of blood on short notice, these medical lights gathered dried blood where animals had been slaughtered. With a good supply of this desiccated gore on hand, the doctor could make a bloody showing in short order, and could perform the reputed impossibility of drawing "blood from a turnip." Before beginning to suck blood from the patient's body, a small bit of this dried blood was put into the mouth. A profuse flow of saliva soon dissolved it; when the doctor could spit out mouthful after mouthful of blood to the admiration and astonishment of the beholders. Thus, we see how brains and genius triumph over ignorance even among savages.

Worms, beetles, bugs, etc. were frequently drawn from the patient's body. Before beginning his operations, the doctor managed to adroitly slip woodworms, maggots, beetles or even a small frog into his or her mouth; and after a brief effort and some mysterious strokings the animals were spit out, living, wriggling proofs of the doctor's skill; whereupon the patient could breathe easily, confident that the cause of his sufferings was removed. To vermin-eating savages, this nasty operation was doubtless less offensive than it would be to civilized people. The vision of "pay" had no doubt much effort in rendering the operation less odious and disgusting. One thing may be said to the credit of the Indians in their management of the sick. They made frequent changes in their position; and, instead of starving the sick, insisted upon feeding them. When an Indian's appetite failed, and he could not take "*muck-a-muck*," he was considered to be in a bad way; and the opinion was generally well founded, for an Indian's appetite usually holds out as long as *Lo* himself [?]; and, if die he must, it is a great consolation to go with a full stomach.

SPIRITUALISM

There seems to have been something among the Indians similar to spiritualism or mesmerism known and practiced for ages. Instead of table tippings and rappings, the mediums, who were always big-medicine men, practiced what was known as "dancing the stick." I [Kuykendall] never witnessed the performance, but have heard it described frequently by a great many eye-witnesses who were present and observed the practice years ago on the Columbia River among the Cascade Indians, and also among the Puget Sound tribes.[77]

An old doctor who became quite famous for his exploits in making sticks dance used to keep five of them for his seances. They are called *tamanowash* sticks. They are about from one and a half to two and a half inches in diameter, and from two to three feet or more long. All [the people, audience at the healing ceremony] being gathered into the lodge and ready for the performance, the old doctor began to sing his *tamanowash* song. After he had sung four times, then any person present was invited to take hold of one of the sticks. As the old man sang and kept time with his hands, the person was jumped about by the stick which began hopping up and down. As the old *tamanowash* man warmed up and sang louder and faster, the stick danced more vehemently and the party [volunteer] holding it was instructed to keep it from moving and hold it still. The more strenuously he tried to resist the dancing, the more violently it hopped up and down and around the lodge. Finally, the stick raised up and jerked up violently the uplifted arms of the one who was trying to hold it. At last being overcome, he fell over in a cataleptic state, holding onto the stick with a death grip. The old *tamanowash* man then stopped his singing and went to the one who had fallen over and stroked him or made some passes over his head when the [cataleptic] rigidity relaxed and the man or woman wakened up as from sleep and was soon all right again. Indians familiar with the performance have described the sensations they felt on taking hold of the *tamanowash* sticks to be almost exactly the same as that experienced when holding the electrodes of a magneto electric battery [sic]. They say their muscles were thrown into a state of powerful contractions so that they cannot let go their hold by any effort of the will (K:27-28).[78]

Very amusing accounts are given of some of the incidents occurring at these seances. Sometimes these *tamanowash* sticks were used in the medicine pow-wows. During the drumming and singing, the stick was laid across the bed in the hands of the patient.

If a cure was to be effected, the stick, while the pow-wow was going on, would raise the sick person up in bed or even pull him up on his feet. In those cases where the imagination plays the greater part in the sickness, and the will power is paralyzed, the power of faith and an excited imagination may do great things towards recovery. A great number of eye-witnesses have testified that, after being danced about for a time at the will of the sorcerer, these sticks would stand or dance about alone, and even remain suspended in the air, nothing touching them. This all sounds very much like the operations of the so-called spiritualists of modern times [among whites].

MOURNING CUSTOMS

In case of the death of an Indian woman's husband, it was the custom for the deceased man's mother to bring the widow a present of a buffalo or elk skin, and seat the bereft daughter-in-law on it, and then cut her hair off a little below the ears. A small bunch of hair was tied together on each side with a buckskin string just above each ear. This was known as the "widow string," and was a badge signifying that the woman was in mourning. The mother-in-law kept the woman's hair during the period of mourning, and when it was over returned it to her. If the husband's mother or some of his clan did not make this present and cut the hair, it was equivalent to telling the daughter-in-law that her marriage into the family again was not desirable. The widow was required to wear the widow strings a whole year without combing her hair. At the end of that time it might be combed out and the strings replaced. Two years was the ordinary period of mourning, during which the strings must be worn; some tribes required three years.[79] She was expected during this time to wear constantly a tight-fitting basket cap woven from grasses, and to paint her face black. At the expiration of the mourning period, the strings were removed, and the woman was a candidate for marriage. While the "widow strings" were worn, no man could show the woman any gallantry; or, if he did, the woman was expected to resent it; and the man was subject to the censure of the chiefs.

Another curious custom that prevailed among the Northwestern Indians was that when a man died his horses were driven up, and their manes and tails were cropped. They said the dead man's hands had stroked the mane and touched the tail. This hair was unclean, and was removed to avert evil consequences from the spirit. This cropping of manes and tails was a kind of badge, also showing to every one that the owner was dead. Horses belonging to women or children were treated the same way. When a man's wife died, his wife's relatives cut his hair and gave him a present of a horse or buffalo robe. This signified their willingness for him to marry into the clan again. As it was an established rule, that when a man married into a clan all subsequent wives were to be taken from that clan, it was a disgraceful affair if the friends failed to cut the hair and make presents as just related. When one of a clan died, all other members, particularly near relatives, were to go through a period of five days' purification by sweating and bathing. During these five days, a widow or widower would not see food prepared. A kind of broth was made and brought; and the mourner was to eat with closed eyes. They were to eat sparingly; and some fasted the whole five days. At the end of this period they ate as usual. The husband's term of mourning was one year; but the mourning of husbands was not so rigidly enforced as that of wives. The Indians explained the five days' sweating and washing to be a purification. The person who had died had looked upon them; they had touched his hands or person; his gaze and touch had contaminated them; and they must get rid of this contamination. In the spring or summer months, they gathered fresh rose leaves and bushes, and bruised them with stones and rubbed them on their bodies, and put the rosebushes upon hot stones in their sweathouses, pouring water on so as to make a strong odor of the rosebush, which was considered cleansing, and had the property of keeping away the spirits of the dead. They had a superstition that newly deceased persons had a desire to return and frequent the old familiar places or touch the living friends.

There was a deathly dread of the spirits of the dead. Immediately after a death, the lodge was swept clean. The Chinooks used to flame burning torches all about the lodge as if driving out flies. These operations would drive out the spirits. To keep away the spirits of the dead, they cast ashes or dust in the air. They say the *tichachie* (spirits of the dead) do not like dust or ashes. For this reason they strew ashes along the way the corpse was carried from the lodge; the *tichachie* would not walk through the ashes.

Immediately after the breath had left the body, a loud wail went up from the friends, the women in particular. In fact, the mourning was mostly done by the women. There was no set formula for the wailing. The expressions were such as," Alas! Alas! O my dear sister!" "O my father! I shall never see you again,!" etc. The mourning was most commonly done early in the morning, just as the sun was coming up. Sometimes almost the whole clan would go out towards the place of sepulture, wailing in the most doleful manner. Generally the old women were the chief mourners. These often volunteered their services at mourning, and usually expected a gift for their performances; and sometimes, in order to make the gift as large as possible, they claimed to have lamented very vehemently and piteously. It often happened that sometime after a death, and when there had been no mourning for a long time, a near friend would break out suddenly in piteous wailing at the sight of a garment or other article of the deceased. The Umpquas formerly put pitch and ashes or pitch and powdered charcoal on their hair while mourning; and, in all the tribes, a woman mourning for a husband deceased was not expected to wash or comb. The more ragged, dirty and slovenly she went, the greater regard she was showing the departed. To wear good clothes, laugh or be cheerful was an insult to the dead, and a certain indication that the person was lacking in respect for the deceased. Widows who did not howl vehemently or constantly enough were considered voluptuous and anxious to marry, and were regarded with contempt. Superstitious fears prevent the tribes east of the mountains from mourning at night.

BURIAL CUSTOMS

The manner of sepulture of the Indians varied. Those east of the Cascades buried the dead. Those on Puget Sound in many places deposited corpses in canoes, putting the body in one canoe and turning another over it, the upper canoe being the smaller. The canoes were propped up two or three feet from the ground. On the [lower?] Columbia River the Indians deposited their dead in houses built of bark or cedar boards of their own making. The corpse was lashed to a post or board and placed in an inclined position until the fluids had drained away; and finally it was placed horizontally. The "dead-houses" were covered over and shut in with care. Islands in the Columbia River were favorite burial places, being more out of the reach of coyotes and other wild animals.[80] Some of the Chinooks used to put dead infants in quiet, still pools of water.

Among all the Indians, whatever mode of sepulture was chosen, much of the deceased person's personal property was placed with or about the body. Pots, kettles, cups, guns, knives, bows and arrows, pipes, articles of clothing and ornament, and money were buried with the dead man or placed about the grave.[81] All utensils had holes punched in them; guns were broken or rendered useless to the living. Clothing was wrapped about the corpse with blankets and robes, and not damaged. The object of breaking or marring property was to prevent theft. The Columbia River Indians were more punctilious in their burial customs than any other of the Oregon or Washington Indians. On the death of chiefs, slaves were formerly killed that they might go into the spirit world to wait upon the master.[82] They were strangled with a cord drawn tightly about the neck, or sometimes tightly bound and lashed to the corpse face to face, touching and left thus to die. Horses and dogs were killed also on these occasions. The notion was that the spirit of the dead man mounted the spirit of the horse; and that, thus equipped, the soul of the deceased rode to the spirit land.

A few years ago among the Yakimas, a certain Indian died; and one of his horses was killed, according to the usual custom. A little while afterwards there was a religious dance held; and a certain old *tamanowash* prophet claimed to have been permitted to look into the other world. He said the dead man had never reached the happy country. His people had committed a grave error because they killed a stallion for the dead man. Instead of bearing his spirit to the Indian heaven, he was roaming around over the earth with poor *Shullaway*,[83] and would forever wander in quest of animals of the opposite sex! This was taken as divine revelation.

A custom that prevailed more or less among all the tribes east of the mountains[84] was that, if a person of a traveling party died, they placed his body upon a scaffold in the air and afterwards removed it to a place of burial. It was the usage of all the tribes to take up the bones of the dead, and clean them and wrap them in new blankets or robes, and rebury them. Sometimes this rehabilimenting was done several times. The river tribes had regular ossuaries where they stowed away the bones of the dead. At the Cascades there formerly was one extensive ossuary.[85] It had been there doubtless for many hundreds of years. Lewis and Clark noticed it when they were on their expedition nearly ninety years ago; and it was then in much better condition than it was sixty years later. It was mostly destroyed when the Oregon Steam Navigation Company built their portage railway at the Cascades. Some of the Indians in the extreme southern part of Oregon about Klamath Lake formerly burned their dead, and burned slaves on the death of a chief.

There is a prevailing idea among the Indians of the Northwest that there is some mystic power or influence connected with the wild rosebush, and that the perfume, though so pleasant to the living, is offensive to the dead. When a person was very sick they generally stuck up rosebushes all around the head of the bed to keep away the spirits. Some of the Indian say the spirits do not like the thorns.[86] The ghosts gather about a sick and dying man, and are beckoning him and trying to steal him away from the living. Ghosts and spirits of the dead hang about graveyards; and Indians have a superstitious dread of such places. It is a prevalent notion that the spirits are particularly active at night. Women will not carry a baby near a graveyard; or, if they do, they put rosebushes all around the papoose board to keep away the ghosts. Spirits of the dead are supposed to have a peculiar love or affinity for little infants, and are always watching an opportunity to snatch the little souls [ones] away.

To eat salmon or berries after touching a corpse, without being purified by the five days' sweating, would be the height of imprudence. The offended salmon would cease to run, the berries would not grow. Food so handled would never digest, would be poison and cause the body to wither away.[87] If a sick person dies, anything he might have happened to spit upon must be burned. The dead are handled by persons who have been inspired by the ghosts, or persons who have the *tlchachie* (ghost) *tamanowash*. If the eyes of a corpse remain open, the spirit is looking back on some member of the family who will soon follow it in death. After death in a lodge, that lodge is always torn down and removed; because the spirit of the dead person will naturally linger about where the body last lay. If a campfire by accident or otherwise be built over a grave, or where a human corpse has lain or blood was spilled in murder, the ghost of the deceased will appear in the flame, and his shadow be seen on the ground near the fire.

At a funeral, all are careful not to drop anything they may have about the person, even a hair; the person dropping it will sicken and die. Leaving a graveyard they never look back, and never point a finger at a grave. These are insults to the dead that will surely be resented. If anyone should by accident sleep where someone was buried, or where someone died, the ghosts of the dead will draw that person's eye or mouth to one side. The distorted mouth and dropped eye caused by facial paralysis, the Indians believe, was always the work of spirits of the dead. The name of this disease in the Klikitat language was about the same as saying "ghost disease." Those who walk over graves or where human blood was spilled and death resulted will have crooked anchylosed knee-joints; the spirit of the deceased will inflict this punishment as a mark of his displeasure. Those who smell the stench of putrid corpses, the Indians believed, were very liable to shrivel up, waste away and die.

Superstition lingers long and dies hard, and is the last relic of barbarism to fall before the march of mental progress. No nation and perhaps even no individual exists today who is wholly free from this clog to reason. The mythic ideas of the ancient Grecians, Romans, and many other nations of antiquity are emblazoned all over our literature. The days of our weeks and months are but the names of mythic heroes that lived only in the imagination of races long since dead. Astronomy, the sublimest science known to man, has crowned the stars with names once borne by hero gods and mythic personages conjured into existence by the imagination of barbarians. The people of our own blood and race are not far enough out of the fogs of superstition to divide the credulity or ridicule the myths of the savages about them. We have only to look back a few centuries to find our own ancestors living in wigwams, clad in the undressed skins of beasts, and as unlettered and superstitious as the North American Indians.

REHABILIMENT OF THE DEAD

Reclothing the dead was an almost universal custom of the tribes of Oregon and Washington, more especially of those along the Columbia River and east of the Cascade Mountains.[88] The Indians about the Cascades, and down towards Vancouver, formerly went in the fall, when the fishing season was over, to the islands up the Columbia River, where their cemeteries and "dead-houses" were, and rehabilimented their dead. They went in boats taking along blankets, buffalo and elk skins, moccasins, beadwork, and whatever fancy or affection might dictate, to put with the bones of their deceased friends. If they arrived at the place in the evening, bringing a corpse to put away in their places of sepulture, or bringing garments to reclothe the dead, they never stopped on the island, but camped on the shore of the river a little distance away. It was their rule to do all handling of corpses in burial, or redressing, in the forenoon, as they believed that at that time the spirits were more quiet, and not moving so freely around in the world. Along towards evening, they believed the ghosts were out around and were more active in exerting their malevolent influences. If they had along a corpse, it was taken some distance from camp, put up out of the reach of wild beasts during the night. When thus camping near the islands containing their cemeteries, they were very superstitious, and dreaded some kind of injury from the spirits of the dead. They had stories of seeing lights in the night-time about the dead-houses, and of hearing the spirits of the dead Indians beating drums and dancing. This was taken as an omen of evil. The spirits were dancing in prospect of meeting someone of the campers, who was soon to die.

On arriving, in the morning, at the place of sepulture, the Indians set off at a little distance, and gave directions as to the reclothing of their dead friends. The work of handling the corpses or bones was done by one man, who had received the *tamanowash* spirit or power from the ghosts. He was called, "*thch'ach-au koot-koot-la*," worker with the dead, or "*klaky-kle'-kle*," turner of the bones of the dead. This old man, for he usually was past middle life, was well paid for these services. While working about the graves or corpses, he pretended to hold communications with the dead, and was heard talking, apparently asking or answering questions. Sometimes he would report that the spirits were offended at the presence of some person or persons of the company, in which case these persons always went away without a second warning, losing no time in their going. The old *klaky-kle'-kle*'s communications were various; and, whatever they were, they were received by the Indians as almost divine revelation. The custom was to scrape off all the decayed animal matter from the bones of the dead, and then to wrap them in blankets, or robes made of the skins of wild animals, putting in such articles as moccasins, knives, beads, pipes, and red pigments for painting the face, etc. The bones, with these articles, were well wrapped up and carefully placed on platforms elevated about two feet in their houses of sepulture. The remains of families were placed side by side, with heads to the west.

The tribes east of the Cascade Mountains, in the bunch-grass country, generally buried their dead. These tribes also rehabilimented their dead, digging the earth out of the graves, cleaning everything away, and wrapping the bones up in blankets or skins of animals, the same as the river tribes. In some cases the reclothing of the deceased was kept up for years; some kept it up every year, others at intervals of from two to four years. Frequently the death of someone in the tribe would be made the occasion of reclothing a relative of the deceased, who had died years previously. Often, in such a case, the old grave was dug out; and the bones of the first were buried with the corpse in the old grave. It was generally believed that putting clothes upon the bones of deceased friends, and articles of use and ornament in the graves, long after their burial, was greatly appreciated by the spirits of the departed, and that these blankets, clothing and trinkets in some way added to the comfort, happiness and respectability of the spirits in the other world. Somehow, the spirit of the material blanket, moccasin, pipe, etc., would go and attach itself to the spirit of the dead. I do not know of any of these tribes that put food in the graves, though this may have been practiced. It was a very common idea that the spirits or ghosts were always hungry; and, while the Indians did not leave food at the graves, as the Chinese do, they, when passing graves carrying any article of food, always threw a little towards the place of burial. An omission to reclothe the dead was considered a mark of a brutish, unfeeling heart; and the neglect was liable to result in some dire visitation from the spirits.

The old *klaky-kle'-kles*, or persons who work among the bones of the dead, say they can hear very distinctly the voices of those recently buried. After some time, the sounds are less distinct; and the voices sound as if the spirits were talking "through their noses." Later on, when the body has nearly crumbled to dust, the tones get down to faint whispers; and, when the last vestige of the bones and body are gone, the voices cease entirely. Many years ago there was a famous ossuary at the Cascades, where bones had been accumulating for ages perhaps. The ruthless hand of civilization has almost obliterated these old landmarks of ancient superstition. However much we may boast of our freedom from superstition, and ridicule the ideas of the Indians, there are yet many whites who, like the "Yankee boy," feel constrained to whistle to keep up courage while passing a graveyard at night.

THE INDIANS' IDEA OF THE SOUL
AND A FUTURE STATE

As has been mentioned, the Indians believe that all objects are of a dual nature, having a soul or spirit-like existence independent of the material form. It is said that some of the Oregon tribes formerly held that the various organs of the body were each endowed with separate souls. Among all the tribes the idea seemed to be that there were really two persons, the spirit or soul, and the body with its animal life, and that the body could exist for some time while the soul was absent. This ghostlike self had the same form and visage as the body. While they believed in a spirit or soul, they do not appear to have thought it was as much a reality as the body. There was a vague, misty unsubstantiality about it that must have been very unsatisfying to their minds. The soul could leave the body and go away in dreams and trances, and could appear as an apparition in places far from the body, with form and features recognizable. In their languages, life and breath or spirit and breath meant the same thing.

A good many if not all of the Indians believed that there were certain shamans or conjurors that could rob them of their souls, and that the body would continue to live on for a longer or shorter time, but that it must soon die. In their so-called doctoring *pow-wows*, the doctors professed to restore the absent soul to its owner, and thus make his recovery to health possible. Another idea quite prevalent among the tribes in Northern Oregon and Washington was that the soul could come back and inhabit some other body. The most northerly tribes bordering upon and reaching into British Columbia thought the soul came back and entered certain birds, fish, or the deer or elk. Others held that the soul came back in the body of infants born to near relatives. It entered the body of a female and appeared in her child. If the child strongly resembled the deceased, then there was no doubt but that he had appeared again; and his name was sooner or later conferred upon it. Some of the tribes in the Northwest held that the deceased could choose in what family he would be born again; and, among the poor and sick or suffering, life was laid down with little regret, believing they might after a while be born into wealthy or honorable families. It was generally believed that the spirits of the dead are out around the world very active and busy during the night, but that in the daytime they stay about graveyards and lonely, dark places. Some held that the dead go into a state of insensibility as soon as the light of day comes on; and that, when darkness broods over the world, their spirits come forth rehabilimented and happy, dancing, feasting and engaging in all kinds of pleasures during the hours of darkness.

Whatever happiness or bliss was attributed to those in the spirit land, there seems to have been a sort of vague dread and much misgiving in regard to it; and their legends show clearly enough that it was the general belief that it would be desirable to have the souls of the deceased return to earth; and that the existence here is really more substantial and desirable than that in the spirit land. Everything goes to show that for some cause there had been a great deal of change going on in the belief of the tribes for some time before the advent of the Whites. Their traditions indicate that the Indians had been traveling and mixing more together than formerly. There is every indication that, at some period back only a few hundred years, the tribes had no horses; and their excursions were limited, and there were greater provincialisms in customs and beliefs than in later times. Formerly each little tribe had its own grounds, lived and died near their birthplaces, and seldom traveled to any extent. Under these circumstances, each had its own legends and myths, and its own particular belief as to the future. Now and for some years back there are found traces of several beliefs mixed in with all the tribes. There was much more independence in thought and difference in religious belief than we have been prone to imagine. There was much more skepticism and tendency to unbelief than we have been taught to look for. Many individuals, when asked about the future state, will say, "I don't know." Some express a doubt as to the immortality of the soul; and some utterly deny it.

Among most of the tribes, there seems to have been a pretty distinct idea of rewards and punishments based on the Indian's idea of right and wrong. In nearly all cases, there was hope held out for relief and final entrance into the happy land. Generally, after an uncertain length of time spent in banishment, the sins of the offender were expiated, and he was permitted to pass in among the good, or was even assisted in. Among no tribes do we find anything like the orthodox fire and brimstone hell; but there are very close representations to the condition of the ancient Tantalus forever tortured with images of everything pleasing to the senses, but which he was utterly unable to grasp. The Chinooks and Klikitats believed in a bright, happy land not very definitely located, where the good were permitted to enjoy themselves in hunting, fishing and every pleasure conceivable to the Indian mind; while the wicked were condemned to wander away in a land of cold and darkness to starve and freeze unceasingly. Some of the Northern tribes say that in the other world there is a dark, mysterious lake or ocean; and that out of this lake there flow two rivers. Up one of the shores there is a beautiful country filled with all manner of berries and game, while the streams abound in fish. Here the good Indian lives in happiness and comfort forever. Up the other river there is a land of frost, darkness, a stony, barren waste, a land of briers and brambles, where the sunlight never comes and where the wicked wander forever in cold, hunger and despair.

The Okanagans have an Indian heaven, and a peculiar kind of hell. Instead of the orthodox cloven-footed, barbed-tailed devil, there is a being in human form with ears and tail of a horse. This fantastic being lives in the pine trees, and jumps about from tree to tree, and with a stick beats and prods the poor souls consigned to his dominions. If among the tribes of the Northwest there is any idea of a heaven in the sky or in some elevated spot in space, it probably was derived from priests or missionaries. In the extreme southern part of Oregon, the Indians represent the happy hunting-grounds as beyond a deep, dark gulf or chasm across which all must pass,—some say on a slippery pole. The good manage to get over, but the evil fall in and reappear upon earth in the form of beasts, insects or birds. One of the most common ideas among the interior tribes was that the spirit land is situated far away towards the south or west. In its journey the soul meets far out on the way a spirit being who understands his life, and weighs all his conduct and actions. If he has been bad, he is sent on to a crooked, wandering road that leads to a land of misty darkness where the soul, forlorn, cold and hungry, forever wanders in despair; while the good are directed along a straight road leading to a country that is bright and beautiful, and abounding in everything the Indian can desire.

These various shades of belief all give expression to that unutterable longing, characteristic of humanity in all ages, to look into the future to unravel the mystery of death, and to solve the problem of man's destiny after he quits this mortal body. In his vain attempts to satisfy the yearnings of his soul after immortality and happiness beyond the grave, men in all lands have invented mythic stories. Death, silence and darkness fill the savage mind with superstitious dread. The most profound and philosophical stand silent in the presence of death. Each tribe or nation of people has its own ideas of heaven; and each pictures what from its standpoint would seem the most happy and desirable condition. No people can picture a heaven superior to the powers of their conception to originate. The Indian's heavenly mansion was a mat-house;—because he had never seen nor thought of anything superior or better. Drumming, dancing, gaming and feasting were the highest conceptions of felicity possible to the Indian mind. Hence he pictured for himself a heaven in which these are the chief pleasures. The river and coast tribes, being accustomed to water and boats, located their heaven on a faraway island; and the spirits were conveyed to the Indian paradise in boats. The prairie tribes, being accustomed to horses as the speediest and best mode of conveyance, sent their dead to heaven on horseback.

We-yal-lup Wa-ya-cika, of Wiley City, Washington. Shaman and chief, the Ahtanum Clan of the Yakimas, d. Dec. 17, 1915. Historical Photograph Collections, Washington State University Libraries.

Histo [Schablo], half *Deschutes* (*Tenino?*) and half *Wasco*, warrior who fought in the Modoc War, 1873. (c. 1911) Historical Photograph Collections, Washington State University Libraries.

Rocks piled up by Indian *Tahmahnawis* hunters on Ahtanum Mountain, nearly opposite Ahtanum City, Washington. Torn down by relic hunters, ruins of one of the finest of the Indian constructed stone heaps can be seen in the foreground, before McWhorter's mount, *Ukut'och-ise* (Wild Eye). L. V. McWhorter photo, July 1918; Courtesy of Mrs. Judith McWhorter Goodwin.

CHAPTER TWO

THE ORIGINS OF SHAMANS' POWER
OR *TAHMAHNAWIS*[89]

At about age twelve, the spirit power quest was undertaken by an Indian youth. The experience was surely fraught with terror for the boy or girl, for spirit beings from which *tahmahnawis* was obtained were everywhere, ghosts were heard in the night, or there were prospects of attack by wild animals from the dark. Taken to a remote spot in the forest or mountains, the youth was given a task to perform. Neither food, water nor sleep was allowed. During the night, as in a dream, an animal in an awesome guise would approach, would speak to the youth, would tell him of his spirit power, would teach him a spirit song, and then depart. Upon return home the youth might tell his parents of his success in acquiring a *tah* spirit, even that of a shaman.

But not until even ten years later would the youth "declare" himself as having a shaman's *tah*, and during the winter's dances with the help of another would attempt to cure. But not all youth acquired *tahmahnawis*, even though they might make numerous attempts. Indeed, one Indian confessed: "But not at all have I seen anything that they call a guardian spirit, I do not know what it is like."[90]

Spirit power was acquired by at least two means. First, the vision quest was perhaps most common. An outstanding example of the vision quest occurs in *"Laux-woptus"* hereafter wherein a vision-questing youth is aroused in the night by the angry rattling of a rattlesnake close beside his head. But when the youth turns his head, not a rattler but an old man, a dwarf perhaps eighteen inches tall, is standing close by.[91] Upon instructing the youth in the rudiments of the *tahmahnawis* power which he would confer on him, the dwarf drops to his belly, and crawls away—a **rattlesnake**. With daylight, the sound of the snake's angry buzzing heard in the night is discovered: a feather caught in the brush and fluttered by the wind.

Still another version of the terrors associated with the   vision quest after *tahmahnawis* is recounted in *"Tahmahnawis* Power—Medicine Man" hereafter. At night a youth falls into an open grave where, against the chill of the night, he must wrap himself for warmth with the rotted wrappings of the dead. Awakened by the drumming/rattling of the dead, he is petrified with fright at the skeleton ghosts of his dead father and grandfather before him. From them the youth receives spirit power to become a powerful shaman.

Second, shamanistic power was also inherited from fathers [not mothers?] according to several shamans in "Bitten on the Trail," also *"Histo's* Narrative of his Father" hereafter. Finally, the demonic *tahs* of the sorcerer are reflected in two narratives which close this chapter.

The narratives and notes hereafter were collected by McWhorter.

1. POWER OF THE MEDICINE MAN, HOW OBTAINED[92]

You know we were talking about the Chief *Wah'k-puch* [rattlesnake], and all the bad things that are crawling on the ground. I will tell you more. Some little Indian boy goes off somewhere one day.[93] These Chief *Wah'k-puch* stop him and tell him what to do, what power they will give him. The *Wah'k-puch* is wise and knows all.

This snake, the Chief snake, decides to kill a person. He calls a council of all the headmen, and they select one of their men to go bite the Indian. No difference where that Indian goes, the snake will find him. [The Indian] cannot get away.

Another animal, the grizzly bear. They kill people and are bad. The grizzly is wise and hard to kill. The power of the grizzly is strong. Some Indians get their power from this bear.

Big owl, all owls, little owls too, they are powerful. The medicine men get power from them. The owl is wise and knows almost everything.[94]

Wolves, coyotes and dogs. They give their power to Indians and the medicine man. The boy or woman, say twenty-five years old [sic], wants to doctor, wants to be medicine man or woman. They tell the people when dancing and singing: "I am singing for a doctor." They tell the people when dancing and singing: "I am singing for a doctor. I will be a doctor in one year. I will doctor anybody free for one year." They doctor free for one year and then they get pay.

We had a strong law. Some doctors are no good—bad and they poison children and people and kill them. The strong law was to kill these bad doctors.

When a man or woman is dying, they will talk plainly. They then tell the words used against them by the bad medicine man who has killed them. They speak just as if they were the medicine man. They may say: "I killed you! I poisoned you with my power. Why did I do it? Why somebody led me to do it!" The dying person will call the name of the one who has caused their death. It is always the doctor. Then the friends or relatives of the dead person kill the bad medicine man. The medicine man does not resist. But if he can get away and stay away for three or five years, he can then return and still be a doctor. They do not kill him then. This was a good law for the Indians. It kept the bad medicine men out of the way.

But when the white man came and made strong laws, we could not use our law against these bad medicine men. Since then many good Indians have been killed by the medicine men, and the white man's law protects them. This is not a good law for the Indians. The medicine man can hurt you or can help you just as he pleases.

2. *TAHMAHNAWIS* POWER—MEDICINE MAN[95]

A young Indian boy was watching a great dance near the Cascades, given by the Cascade Indians[96] one night, and late in the night left the dance grounds and started for home. His path led over a high piece of ground in the timber. Along this trail there was an Indian burial ground, and unknown to the boy his mother and friends had that very day exhumed the

bodies of her dead husband, the child's father, and also
the body of his grandfather, for the purpose of
transferring them to another burial ground.[97] The boy
fell into one of the graves which had been left open and
could not climb out of it. He did not know the nature
of his prison-pit. He felt upwards and found that
despite his most strenuous efforts he could not escape.
It was cold and he thought: "I will die here." He felt
about and found a piece of a blanket, the soiled
wrappings of the dead, and drew that about his
shoulders and settled down for the night.

After remaining thus for some time, he heard
Indian voices in song, accompanied by the rattling
pounding of sticks on wood, after the custom of the
"helpers" of the Indian medicine man. The voices and
noise grew louder and drew nearer to him. Presently
it was just back of him, and eventually was at his side.
Then it was on both sides of him. The rattling of the
"helpers" sticks and the wild weird song was continued
for some time. Then the boy saw what it was that was
with him. He saw his skeleton father and next-father
[grandfather] standing on either side of him, singing.
They were shaking their bony hands, striking and
rattling their fleshless fingers, and it was this noise he
heard instead of the pounding of sticks on timber as
first supposed. Then the skeleton parents from the
spirit world spoke to the boy and instructed him in the
art of healing certain diseases. He would become a
great "medicine" man if only he obeyed their rules and
instructions. He was then shown how to make use of
the fragments of burial sticks still in the deserted
grave, how to brace them against the sides of the
cavern and climb by them to the upper air. This was

at break of day and the boy following the instructions of his unearthly visitors, soon escaped from his gruesome prison.

The influence of that night's supernatural visitation never left the boy during the succeeding years. He grew up under its halo, if such it may be termed, and in due time became the powerful "medicine man" as promised. The age of tutelage and instruction generally extends to, or near the fortieth year of life, or to just past middle age, and it was at this age that this lad of the deserted grave entered on his successful career as "medicine man." He has practiced in the [Puget] Sound Country, the Warm Springs, Umatilla, and the Yakima [territories].

I have seen this man at his incantations over a very sick man. Aside from suction with the lips, all was purely of the occult. I saw him produce blood containing small atoms of clotted and seemingly unnatural blood from the pit of his patient's stomach by suction.[98] His performance was accompanied by the usual invocational *tahmahnawis* songs, with the beating of sticks on a board by a number of "helpers." He could not speak the Yakima language, but used Chinook[99], his "repeater" translating it into Yakima[100]. There is doubtless some virtue in his methods, but his stronghold is in the superstitious credulity of the Indians. His "medicine" was administered at night and occupied three hours' time. The patient seemed comforted, if nothing more, by the wild weird process. *Is* there anything in it?

3. *LAUX-WOPTUS*[101]

A small *Yakima* boy was sent into the hills one night in quest of *tahmahnawis* power. For a time he wandered about or cowered in terror of the darkness and lonely solitude. At length overcome with drowsiness and fatigue, he fell asleep. In the night he heard close to his head, a vibrant buzzing not unlike that of the rattlesnake. He glanced over his shoulder, but instead of a rattler, he saw an old man, a dwarf, rise up out of the ground. The strange being stood not over eighteen inches in height, with long white hair flowing to his waist. He accosted the boy, telling him that he would be his guiding spirit through life, conferring on him his own power and strength. After delivering this message, along with certain rules to be observed, the white-haired dwarf dropped to his belly and crawled away: **a rattlesnake**.

The lad was now fully awake. He looked! There was neither old man nor rattler in sight. But the mysterious buzzing continued. Investigation disclosed a solitary feather, lodged in a shrub and fluttered by the wind. The feather vibrating, struck a twig, produced a "purr" not unlike that of a disturbed rattlesnake. Securing the feather, the boy carried it to his parents and informed them how he came by it.

The parents said: "It is good! The boy's name shall be *Laux-woptus*: 'one feather.'"

Laux-woptus is still living at this writing (1921).

4. STONE HEAPS OF THE *N-CHE-WANA*[102]

Long time ago Indian boys were sent to
mountains by their father, or next of kin. Maybe it is
an old man, a good hunter, a great warrior or medicine
man, who sent the boy. That boy must stay two or three
days and nights in a lonely place. He must not drink
water, he must not eat food. He must pray and call on
the Ruling Spirit. He must not sleep; but after a time
he will fall down and sleep. He then sleeps; hears
strange things. The boy piles up stones so that his
people will know that he has been there. Perhaps such
are the stoneheaps you saw on the summit of the big
boulders along the *n-Che'-wana*.

I, myself, was in the mountains four times.[103]
It makes the boy honest; makes him obey his parents.
It makes him think of the future life. It is good for the
boy to go to the mountains. He must go when about the
size of that boy [indicating a lad twelve or fifteen years
of age].

5. THOSE STONE HEAPS[104]

Those stone heaps you ask about! They were
made this way. Years ago the old Indians would send
their children, their little boys when about ten and
twelve years old, to the mountains to stay seven days
and seven nights. The boy made a pile of stones and
then sat down. He must not eat; must not drink water.
He must not sleep at night. But when *may-wik*
[morning] comes, he can sleep sitting this way
[assuming recumbent position]. The boy must think
about the things that his father has told him. It will

make him good. Then, when he sees something out there in the night, that thing will talk to him. It will tell him what to do. The guidance is good. It makes the boy strong! It goes with him through life.

Sometimes there is an old man who has lost all his people. He feels lonely; he is sad. He goes up on the mountain somewhere. He builds up stones. He sits there and cries, for he is alone in the world. In this way were many of those stone-heaps made. The white man should not tear them down.

6. SOURCE OF A *TAHMAHNAWIS*

An old Indian of the Ellensburg contingent of the Yakimas had a *tahmahnawis* of the *Mum-ma-tah*: "next to the slide rocks," the name of a small brown bird known as the Rock-wren which is the deadly enemy of all snakes, including the rattler. Alighting on the neck of the reptile, the bird strikes its sharp beak deep into the back of the head of its victim, killing it almost instantly. The Indian in question killed a rattlesnake and, opening it, would detach the two fatty portions adhering to the backbone and swallow them. The *Mum-ma-tah* had instructed him to do this as one of the obligations exacted for its services and guarding *tahmahnawis* power.

7. *TE-CHUM, TAHMAHNAWIS*
OF THE MEDICINE MAN[105]

The *Te-chum' mah*, the dwarf spirit-people living about Fish Lake, Lake Keechelus and the heavily timbered peaks and summit of the Cascades,[106]

occasionally confer their power on the medicine man.
The recipient of such gift is endowed with a faculty
enabling him to understand the inarticulate language
of an infant. The *Te-chum'* speaks to the medicine
man through the baby.

Not many years ago, Jacob, an aged medicine
man of the Kittitas Valley, possessed a *tahmahnawis*
of the *Te-chum'*. He became renowned for his ability
to take from a child its thoughts and set it crazy. He
could make a newborn baby talk. Let a mother pass
before his eyes with her infant, even though she
immediately carried it away, that young prodigy would
talk. Unless the charm was broken by the spell-binder,
the baby soon died. Some times the medicine man
would sit silently, saying nothing while the child
talked. It was in such cases that the mother knew her
baby would die. At other times the old man would,
before going his way, speak to the mother: "I will save
your child. I hear it talking to the *Te-chum' mah*."

Whenever the medicine man spoke in that
way, the mother knew that her child was safe; that it
would pass securely through the enchantment.

Knowing the language of the *Te-chum' mah*,
and possessed of their power, the necromancer could,
if so inclined, avert the threatened demise of the
afflicted little one.

8. KILLING OF *TAH-MAH TO-TAN-IE* ("SPREADING HAIR"), A MEDICINE MAN OF THE *WO-WATCH-WATCH* TRIBE[107]

This happened on Rock Creek when I was a
young woman, some thirty years ago. A man died, and

the medicine men who doctored him said that a certain medicine man, who had not doctored him, had killed him. This medicine man was a good man, but *Yal-lup*, the brother of the dead man, and *Black Wolf*[108], both of the *wo-watch-watch* tribe, determined to kill this accused medicine man. The medicine man slept with a six-shooter at his head every night, and the two men had no gun(s). The medicine man always got up early and went to look after his horses.

One morning after he had left the tepee, *Black Wolf* and *Yal-lup* came and asked his wife for the man's gun, telling her that they wanted to shoot a robin in a tree close by the door. She gave them the gun and they went away without shooting the bird.

They came upon the medicine man and shot him three times, all the loads they had in the gun. The medicine man was a swift runner and often outran horses in a good long race. He could outrun all the young men of the tribe. He ran, all shot through the upper part of the body and the blood streaming down. He was getting away from the two men who were on horses, and one of them said: "Lasso him with the rope! He will get away from us!" So they threw the rope and caught him.

They tied him to a tree and stoned him. They stoned him all over, but could not kill him. He said: "Do not hit me more. I cannot live now. Let me alone, for I will die." But they kept on and finally struck him on the cheekbone below the eye. Then he screamed— the only time he cried out—and was dead. They thought that if they had not hit him on that bone he would not have died—could not have killed him.

In the Wasco tribe, if a man killed a medicine

man, he had to pay the widow, or his children or nearest relatives, for the loss. Pay [was] in horses, dried salmon, blankets or other goods.

CHAPTER THREE

ACCOUNTS BY SHAMANS
DESCRIBING THEIR HEALING POWERS
WITH CORROBORATIVE
STATEMENTS BY PATIENTS

Two famous Yakima shamans are recalled here, expecially from McWhorter's first-hand account of *Nah-schoot*, heard during the night of July 10, 1910, also *Smat-louit*. Although both men and women might become shamans, in fact men predominated. Spirit power obtained by a vision quest, or else inherited was generally feared, but a shaman's life was insecure. His power could be lost by talking about it, as happened when *Histo* explained of his power in "The Source of *Histo's* Power as a Warrior;" or by being neglectful, careless with his magic. And his life could be threatened by grief-stricken relatives of a patient who had died, forcing the shaman to flee into exile, or to suffer death.

Causes of illnesses which the shaman professed to cure included, first, the **disease projectile**. As with the description of the curing ceremony on pages 16-17 above, a cure was effected by extracting from the patient's body a"disease-causing object." The shaman might even hold up to his assembled audience something representing what he had removed from the patient. **Spirit possession** was another cause of illness which the shaman sought to remedy. Indeed, causes of illness or death from spirit possession are numerous here. Due to an invasion of a patient's body by an evil spirit, sickness occurs in narratives nos. 7, 11, 12, 26, 38, 39, 40. Of special interest is Elgin V. Kuykendall's recollection of his father treating the very ill brave afflicted with spirit sickness on pp. 25-26 above. **Soul loss** was perhaps another ailment treated by the shaman, but this we cannot substantiate.

Specialization among the shamans can be perceived in this chapter. First, by his own admission and also the praise of several patients, *Nah-schoot* employed his spirit power to cure Indians of alcoholism. Second, both *Wan'-tah*, also *We-yal-lup Wa-yi-cika* here and in Chapter Four had received their spirit power from the rattlesnake, and so were skilled at dealings with that serpent: at healing snakebite, at handling angry rattlers. Third, the medicine man Jacob was able to avert death of newborn infants threatened by the *Te-chum' mah*. Fourth, *Wal-a-musk'kee* had the special power through nighttime dreams to locate the lost graves of the dead that they might be exhumed, and reblanketed.

Besides healing the sick, shamans possessed other, marvelous powers. First, they were reputedly able to **control the weather**. An example of the shaman smoking, causing a storm appears in No. 21 "A Boy Bitten By a *Wah'k-puch*." Second, **prophecy** was no small part of a shaman's lore. In "A Shaman and His Patients, The Revelations of *Nah-schoot*...," the shaman repeats/recalls a prophesy of the coming of the white man along with his astounding technical devices: the axe, the sailing ship. Third, **prophetic dreams** were still another likely power of the shaman. Examples of such powerful dreams include the warning dream dreamed by *Chow-yah-les* of *Sam-a-lee-sack*, famed bear hunter whose preferred hunting method was to enter the winter den, and knife the animals to death: "There is trouble ahead. There came to me last night a bad dream. I saw a great bear standing erect, dancing. Singing and dancing, he stretched out his arms all red with blood, and said to me, 'See this blood, all red from the heart. It is the blood of one of you hunters. I did this to one of you.' Danger is hiding along our trail. A *tahmahnawis* bear is waiting for us somewhere.[109] [And so it happened a grizzly awaited.] And in "A Lurking *Wah'k-puch* Forestalled" here, a prophetic dream warns an individual of a rattlesnake which lay in their path that day, which would surely bite someone. Finally, a **hunting** *tah* was still another power given some shamans which enabled them to direct hunters to the place where game might be found, as in No. 34, "*Tahmahnawis* Power;" also No.35 "The Owl as a Guide of the Hunter in Quest of Deer" below.

9. A SHAMAN AND HIS PATIENTS, THE REVELATIONS OF *NAH-SCHOOT*: ("SOUND," OR "NOISE"),[110] AND *SMAT-LOUIT*

In my boyhood days, I have seen my older people.[111] I learned what they were doing, what they believed. Of course, when young, I believed what was told me; but I did not understand why they did those things. But I had [preferred] to take that way. My people believed that when we die, if our spirits are cleaned from all sins, we go to the place which is the

Indian's Heaven.

In time, I grew up and became a man. I supported myself. After that, the people, my friends who came before me, showed me liquor. They started me drinking. But after I got started drinking, I worked hard, I had money. I felt pretty good with it [whiskey]. I wanted more. I put my hand into my pocket, and found money there. I said to myself: 'This money is no body's but mine. It is neither my father's, nor my mother's money; and if I spend it, nobody can say anything about it.'

It was then that I became a drunkard. I followed nothing else. After this, I could not remember what the old people had told me, had preached to me. I think that I was about seventeen years old when I began this drinking. From then, I never followed any thing good, *Sapalwit* [Sunday] and weekday were not different to me. I remembered not what had been told me by the old people. I got about as bad as anybody could get. I followed along that line, fighting, and doing everything bad that is caused by drunkenness. But one thing I never did, was to steal horses. Nor did I kill anybody, nor use any instrument against the people in violence.

When I was thirty years old, I quit drinking. I am thirty-eight now. As long as I followed drink, I lost my children all the time. I did not know why my children died. I lost nine children. In all my days, while I was doing these things, I did not think of any thing seriously. But now, after all these years, I see into it—I was drinking the bad stuff. The children are different—they are clear of everything bad. But by me having this bad stuff in me, it interfered with the children and they died.

I had a wife, and a baby about seven months old. My wife took sick. This was in August, 1901. I think she was sick four months. The baby took sick after this. It did not last long. It was nearing Christmas, and the baby died first. The mother died about eight days before Christmas. I first buried my baby. A few days afterwards I buried my wife. I loved my wife, my children.

In about one week I went to the house where we had lived, myself, wife and children. I opened the door and went in. Of course my mind was strong. I looked around. I look where my wife had been, I looked for them all. After I had looked everywhere, I felt sad, felt badly about it. Then I cried out; I knew not myself: "I wish that I could die, could go where my wife and children are. There is no use for me to stay here alone. My wife, my children are all dead."

I wished that something would kill me—I would kill myself—then my spirit would go where they were, and I could see them. I thought that I would then be free from sin, that in death my spirit would go on the same trail as spirits of other people, wherever the spirits go.

But after this, I found that my body was not purified enough for my spirit to go to my wife and children—where their spirits had gone above. That is what we think. Some who are bad think that they are good; that their spirits are clear when they are not. There is a big power, a *tamaniwit* [law] which rules above where our spirits go. My mind was lost; I fell to the ground. After I fell, I was sound asleep. It was nighttime.

When daylight came, I heard a person saying, calling me by name! *"Nah-schoot! Nah-schoot!"*

I could not see the person calling.[112] I heard the person say: *"Nah-schoot!* Your body is not clean enough to come up here. This is not the time for you to die, not the time for you to come up here." Then that [person/deity] showed me my body; I could see myself. Now when I had become a drunkard, every bad thing that I had done, fighting, roaming around on *Sapalwit*, he made me to see. All these bad things, all of my life; what I had done in this world. I was made to see.

I heard him say: "From this time on, you must clean your body, have your spirit purified. You will do this. When you have cleaned and purified enough, then you may die, may come here and see your wife and children. If you do not do this, clean your body and spirit enough, your spirit will never come here, nor will you see your wife and children."

I heard the voice say: "I will stop all your bad feelings about your children and wife. I will give you a rule to go by. When I give you this rule, when you see it as I make it to you, which every way I show you my ruling, you must do. I will make no mistake or change."

"First, you must eat no more of that which troubles your body, which bothers your mind." (Here *Nah-schoot* proceeded to fill his stone pipe and light it before proceeding.)

Then I found the power which was given me to cure people in any case of sickness. I could cure and purify them. I was helped by the person who is above this earth. I was helped by him. He gave me a rule to go by, gave me strength, gave me power. Now I have turned around with this power, given me from above for the weaker people; to cure them of all sickness, all bad habits; to get their bodies free from all badness.

From this time on, I got along easily; my living and my home. He [deity] gave me a trail to go by [on].

He [deity] showed me: "Now you follow this line. Do not get off, but go as you are told. If you follow this line, you can correct other works for your brothers and sisters."

After I got this ruling, I have never gone out of my way [astray], nor have I tried any drop of liquor. I found out at that time, that the Indians have not just one belief. Some believe a little different from others. Some believe, and follow the war dance, who believe in no god. The early people who believed in god, their rules were strict. They would have no laughing or other bad things going on during their worship meetings.[113]

A long time before the Whites discovered this country, there were no telephones, no writing nor correspondence among the Indians. In those days, one man became as myself. He heard some thing and was given a ruling. He did as he was told. There were many, many Indians. He sent out word for them all to come to him. They came. He began to tell them all about your White people who were to come. This was long before any White people had been seen.[114]

The Indian who was given the ruling, said to the people: "You will not do this any more—split timber with elk-horn. These pale people will come and bring implements to work with. They will have some thing to cut the trees. It is flat. They will strike one blow and the tree will come down."

Everything that the White man had, this man foretold about. He said they would have a big canoe. The Indians held meetings. They had men counseled. They talked about these things; nor did they eat. They told other tribes of the things so strange to them. This was the way of the earlier people, how they done [did].

Now from the time these things came to me, I believed that if all people would believe something of this, would keep their children from all bad habits, direct them by these rules, all would be good. I am of younger growth, a young man. The people think that I know not much. Since the time this *tahmahnawis* was given me, I have followed it just as I was told. Since I have followed this law [or ruling], the Indians and my white friends do not fear me. They have no trouble with me. I now wish that all my friends, as my brothers and sisters, would keep this ruling with me, stay by it as I have. If my brothers would follow the words as I give them, follow them correctly, it would be something to help them; something from above, from where I was told.

I think there is only one creator for all different tribes of this world, whites or reds. Some time after this [creation] different languages were given to the different tribes, whites and reds. Now if we do not get along well between all tribes—whites and reds—if we interfere strongly, the creator will make a change. I, *Nah-schoot*, have found out that if the people drink and steal, if they do not follow rules given their fathers and mothers—if in some places, in some countries they are getting along too badly—it [the place or country?] will be destroyed, either by fire or by water. Maybe some town or country will be destroyed. We can see ourselves; if we get too bad, something happens. People are killed by fire, or are drowned. We know that the Creator may destroy us, may change the world.

Now in my mind is this. I do not like any trouble with my white friends; nor do I interfere with them in any way. I always want to do right by them if I can. If the whites would be friendly with the Indians, do everything friendly and right by them, we might get along better. If both Indians and whites would follow this up, be friendly and not interfere with each other in any way, the Creator would know this, and by doing right, nothing bad would happen to us.

I hear that many towns have been destroyed by fire, and some with water. I do not say for all the people to join in my belief. I do not see, nor tell anybody that one belief is better than another. I do not ask them to join any belief, nor do I think that one is bad, or worse than another. We have one Creator, and there are different beliefs, but I believe that all are [have] some good, one in the other.[115]

Now when I give my body treatments, I want no liquor around. I show that I am not to be with the whites, or act their ways. I have long hair; I act in natural Indian ways. I do not follow up the ways we have in our religious meetings only on *Sapalwit*, [but] I follow it [them] every day. But only on *Sapalwit* do I tell my people what to do, how to be and the best way for us. I think that if all our boys would make homes, get some thing to eat, make a living and be content, it would be good. If our boys would leave whiskey alone, I would be glad. In these days it is different from old times. People must raise vegetables. They cannot now go hunting and fishing for a living. That is done away with. At my home I never dress up during the week. I am always working hard for my living, for [my] home. That is the way all children should be taught, how to get along. Should some young man and young woman do well from my talks, I would be glad. With these new bodies, no liquor should be used by either Indians or whites. This is all.

To an interrogation *Nah-schoot* answered: "No! I never was taught anything of christianity. This is all that I will tell tonight. [It was two o'clock A.M.]

I then asked if *Nah-schoot* had derived his curative and prophetic powers from any bird or animal.

The interpreter consulted the "medicine man," and explained: *Nah-schoot* got the most of his power from the lightning. A great storm was raging when he was alone in his desolate home. It was the voice of the spirit of the thunder which spoke to him and gave him the guide to go by. There are things which he cannot tell; for should he do so, his power would leave him. Now I [William Charley] will give you one instance in my own life, but there are other things I have seen and heard, that I will not tell. In this case, it makes no difference; for I have already told it and thereby lost the power that otherwise would now be mine.[116]

When I was a little boy living with my parents on [the] Lewis River, Clark County, this state [Washington], I was sent a short distance from the house to a spring in some bushes, to bring a bucket of water. As I reached the spring, I saw *whish-hoy* [blue jay] sitting in the top of a tree which grew there. The bird immediately flew from its perch towards me. When it was about half way to the ground, its wings became two blue blankets spread out. When it lit near me, it was a good sized man. I remember exactly how he looked and all about his dress. He wore an old-fashioned blue army cap, had on a blue shirt and blue breeches. He wore leggings and leather boots.

He began talking to me, and said: "Are you in a hurry? If you are not in a hurry, we will have some fun."

I said: "No! I am not in a hurry, but you are too big. There is no one here to play with me."

He said: "Sit your bucket down." I did so.

He began to say funny things to me. I laughed so that my parents heard me in the house. They heard me talking and laughing, but knew not what I was doing, or to whom I was talking. After a time he told me to take a drink. I did as told. He then went to the spring and drank.

He said that if I wanted to go home, I could do so; whenever I wanted to go home, I could do so; but whenever I wanted fun, to come there and he would come also.

I filled my bucket and started home. I saw the man spread his blankets and fly upwards. When he reached the top of the tree, he was a blue-jay. I went home and thought [it?] so funny that I told my people about it, all that was said. I never saw the stranger again. Had I not told anything about our meeting, I could to this day hear the *whish-hoy* talk in my own language and could understand. He would have given me his power to do things. This is the reason that no Indian will tell of these things. I have some power with which to help my people, of which I will not tell. But it is not from the blue jay. If I had not told of what the blue-jay said to me, I would now consider him as my brother. I would not hurt or kill him. As it is, I can kill him. No Indian will kill the animal which talks to him and gives him its power. All Indians get some such power from some animal, bird or living creature; sometimes from inanimate object. It may be from a grasshopper or other insect. Often, power is derived from more than one animal or object. These guide us and tell us how to live and do.

10. TESTIMONY OF INDIANS TREATED BY *NAH-SCHOOT* FOR DRUNKENNESS AND OTHER EVILS[117]

A. THE WORDS OF *SI-HOL-TUX* OR CHARLEY *SCHILOO*, BLACKSMITH

I will tell you a short story [an account] about myself; how I had followed my life before I was treated by *Nah-schoot*; how I became a brother of his. Before treatment, I wished that something would stop my bad habits. I tried everything for myself. I went to the Methodist church, thinking that probably if I learned something of their teachings to their people, it would help me from my bad habits. I heard the preacher telling his belief, but as quick as I left the church, I would forget all that he said. I would go to town, get whiskey, and do many bad things. Sometimes I would take my family to town and then come home by myself, leaving them anywhere. Drink left me crazy.

About this time I heard of *Nah-schoot*'s power

to stop this drink habit, and that he had cured many. I thought to myself: "I wish that I could see this man."

Soon, I heard that he had come to this reservation. I had a gallon jug of whiskey at my house. I hid this whiskey and went to see *Nah-schoot*. I met him. I said to him: "I have come to see you. I have a bad home now. I have a drunken habit in my home, and nothing to stop me."

Nah-schoot walked up to me and shook hands with me. He said: "I will come and see you."

He came to my house. I still had that gallon whiskey hid. He gave me his treatment. I used to think nothing could stop my drinking. I think it is now five years since he cured me, and I have not, since then, touched any liquor. From that time I have believed that he has the power to stop all these things, provided anyone takes up with him and does as he tells them.

From that time I looked after my home and did right by my family. I fixed things up in the right way to live. Now there is nothing to bother my home. I believe that he is telling the truth when he says that something from above told him what to do; how to do for his brothers and sisters. Anyone following his rulings, they will be helped out by something from above. After I followed up his rules, I was helped; and it seems that I cannot help doing as he says, for I believe he tells the truth and that something has directed him what to do.

This is the way it is to us. The Whites have things in writing which probably have not been shown to you. But someone comes to you with this writing and you read it and learn something that you had never known before. That is the way of this, although we have no writing. There is something which sees us all the time from somewhere; who created this world and created the people. If we do wrong against His ways, sometime He will correct our ways and give us a ruling to go by; give us the right way to take care of our bodies. I believe that *Nah-schoot* is His messenger.

All this comes to me, to my head so clear, that I believe if we follow natural ways, as the Creator put us here, all will be well. This is all.[118]

B. THE WORDS OF *SCHU-PLI-HI-HIT* (ENGLISH NAME: THOMAS CHARLEY), A COLUMBIA RIVER INDIAN

In my days, after I grew nearly to manhood, I commenced the use of intoxicating liquors. After I got started so far, it [liquor] got a strong hold on me and I used it regularly. It seemed that I could not stop, nor could anyone stop me from the habit. Now this man, *Nah-schoot*, got hold of me and gave me treatment and took the bad habit from me. He took all the whiskey from my system. After taking treatments and doing as he directed, I found that it changed me. I stopped drinking and got along better from that time on. Since that day, I think that he is a brother of mine, and all my people became a brother of his. I believe that he is as much to them as to me. We think that we are all brothers and have one father for all. This is all.

C. THE WORDS OF *SUM-MOT-KIN*
(ENGLISH NAME: ELIJAH ELIX),
A KLICKITAT INDIAN

I was a boy when I came to this country, and was raised here. I became a young man and I heard the old people tell the young people where the man [a prophet?] was from who told of the coming of the white-skinned people with their strange implements. *Nah-schoot* has told you of this. The words of the old people have never parted from me. Right across the road from the White Swan Post Office [the town of White Swan, Washington] is where I was raised. I was going to the Methodist church and I heard their preacher tell their belief. I heard the words; yet, still, I had in my mind the story told by these old people. I could not forget it. I have heard others tell of this religion, and it seems to me that I cannot hear anything better than told by my old people. For this reason, I would not join any other belief.

I, *Sum-mot-kin*, I never followed any drink habit until eight snows ago. I used whiskey and have used it mostly from that time on. Well, it is this way. When I lost my wife and lost my home, I could not forget from feeling bad. That is why I used so much whiskey; for then I could forget my troubles. I kept drinking until I got another woman. Still, after I had lived with this wife for some time, I could not stop drinking. She tried to stop me and would get mad. I finally got drunk and gave her a beating. For some time after that I could not stop. Then *Nah-schoot* came to me and treated me and gave me rules to go by.

What I had been told by the old people was in

my mind until I used whiskey, when all was forgotten and I remembered their teachings no more. It was lost to my mind until *Nah-schoot* treated me and worked the intoxicating liquors from my system. Then what I had once heard from the old people, he told to me and everything came back to me clear. It came back to me as natural as I had learned it many snows before. It is now three snows since I quit drinking. Since then my mind has not been troubled. I have not had trouble as when I was drinking.

You have seen our people and been with them during the Spring Feast at Billy Stayhi's where they eat the new food. Since I have followed the rule given me by *Nah-schoot*, the people gather in my home as at Stayhi's. I follow the same mode of living, the same belief. I have no "long house" as at Stayhi's, but they come to my home. Ever since my treatment, I cannot let the belief go, nor can I help following in that way. This is all.[119],[120]

D. *NAH-SCHOOT'S* DESCRIPTION OF THE INDIAN HEAVEN AND HELL

I cannot say that I am right and without fault. If I make a mistake, I may not go up to the good place. I may make a mistake and not know it, and then I will go to the bad place. We cannot tell how we get there. We will know nothing, but we must go through a single door where all is bad and everybody crying. There is no help for it. We cannot help ourselves. We must be good if we get [would go] to the good place. If I wrong any of my people, then I will go to the bad place. If I do good all the time and help my people, then I will go to the good place for all time. This is all that I will say to you now, but you will see my work tonight and we will get more witnesses to what I have done, curing my people of drink.

E. FURTHER TESTIMONY OF SOME OF THE PEOPLE TREATED BY THE MEDICINE MAN, *NAH-SCHOOT*:

THIRD PATIENT—WOMAN:

I found that I had sickness in my leg. I could not travel very well. I was on the trail. Some man headed me off, and I could not follow it.

FIFTH PATIENT—MAN

I saw the same as I did yesterday. Right back of my head was blackness. I looked eastward and I saw daylight. I saw part of the daylight, and that is all.[121]

11. INCIDENTS IN *SMAT-LOUIT'S* CAREER AS MEDICINE MAN[122]

While [McWhorter was] riding with an educated Christian Indian on the Yakima Reservation, April 28, 1912, an Indian was observed approaching on horseback in the distance. "Dr. *Smat-louit!*" replied my companion, who recognized the aged "medicine man" from afar.

As we met, the younger Indian saluted in the Yakima tongue: "Good morning, Tom (by which Christian name he is known)."

The old man retorted: "Do not talk to me like that when I am mad. I will not stand it."

My companion looked surprised, if not actually frightened. "Well! I did not know that you were that way. I was only speaking to you."

The two Indians exchanged a few words in which seemingly the "medicine man" was partially placated.

After [the old man] passed on, the younger Indian, in response to my inquiry as to the trouble said: "That old fellow is a bad man, and if it was not for the laws of the white people, we would hang him. One time he came to my house early in the morning. He was bad and talked mean. We treated him well, fed him and his horse. When he left, he said to me: 'You will be following me in two or three days.'"

This scared my wife and she asked me what he meant by such words.

I answered: "Do you know what he said? He meant that I would be after him for one of our children. He has done something to our children and one of them will be sick. He expected me to come for him to doctor our child and get pay of some horses or cattle for doing it."

In two days from that time, our little girl baby grew sick and died. She was about two years old and could talk. Just before she died, she repeated the words spoken by *Smat-louit*: 'You will be following me in two or three days.'

"*Smat-louit* killed my child. I am telling you, McWhorter," he added earnestly, "if it was not for this [Roman] Catholic religion of mine, I would have killed the damned son of a cuss as we did in tribal days. All the Indians are afraid of him. He can do you lots of harm."

Smat-louit holds communion with the little *Wah-tee-tas*, the "ancient people" who painted the pictures on the cliff in the Naches Gap.[123] These spirit-people of the cliff, *Smat-louit* can send [his spirit] into the body of anyone he chooses, and he alone can remove this spirit. The following was told me by the husband of the woman affected.[124]

Smat-louit caused serious illness to my wife, and I said to her, "I just as well go pay *Smat-louit* a good price to cure you. And if he does not cure you, he will go up in smoke. I will put dynamite under him and blow him to hell."

My wife said: "My husband, do nothing like that."

I told her that I would unless he cured her. She was worth more to me than anything else, and I agreed to pay *Smat-louit* a cow and a calf, and three horses if he would cure her. He had placed one of those pictures you see painted on those rocks over her face, and at times she could not see. He had also put one of the spirits in her body. He kept working a little with her for three days, but she did not get any better.

I said to him: "Why don't you take that thing from her face and draw the bad spirit from her body? Do you want me to pay you more?"

Then he got ashamed and said: "No! I do not want you to pay me more. I will take it away now."

He than began to work in a good way and soon my wife was well. I gave him the stock promised and was satisfied. *Smat-louit* is a bad medicine man. He talks to the spirits inhabiting the *Puh-tuh-num*" (painted or marked rocks).

12. THE DREADFUL "MEDICINE MAN"

A remarkable instance of the dread in which "medicine men" are held came under my observation in April 1912. A chief of the Yakimas, also a Methodist minister, came to my house and complained of not feeling well.[125] There had been some tribal trouble, and some of the head men had become estranged from each other.

When leaving for home, the Chief said: "I have never felt this way before. Some of the Indians do not like me, and they talk all over the Reservation and say bad things about me. These words go like arrows through the air and do harm. The white people do not understand these things, but they are true."

"*Sluskin* is a medicine man and he does not like me. He said that he and *Lesh-hi-hit* killed *Stick Joe*, the Indian scout for the government in the Yakima War. They killed him with bad *tahmahnawis*. *Lesh-hi-hit* got scared and said afterwards that they did not kill him. *Sluskin* is bad *tahmahnawis*. It is Indians' way, and I am telling you this if anything happens. I never felt this way in my life."

But the Chief recovered and is still living. Chief *Sluskin* has often laughed when told by me of the dread in which he is held by some of the Indians. He denies any occult power as a "medicine man."

CHAPTER FOUR

THE RATTLESNAKE AS
SHAMAN'S SIMPLE

The rattlesnake was the source of very strong spirit power, and was especially feared by the Yakimas.[126] Possessing the rattlesnake *tahmahnawis*, the shamans, *Wan'-tah* and *We-yal-lup Wa-ya-cika*, had varied powers with which to deal with the serpent. First, such a shaman might "doctor" snakebite by simply squeezing from a swollen limb the "infecting" venom. This may well have been but a liquid "disease projectile," for the shaman observes in narratives No. 21 and 22: "I pressed my hands on both sides of the swollen arm like this [stroking slowly down the arm to affected thumb]! Poison is like water. It leaked out." Second, if he was bitten, the shaman was relatively invulnerable to the effects of the serpent's venom. Third, such a shaman was empowered to hear even at a distance serpents talking one with another, and thus to stymie their plotting against people. Or, fourth, when a rattler was about to bite an Indian, the shaman might intercept the serpent. After talking to the snake [the snake comprehending], the shaman would banish the rattler, send it crawling to a distant area out of harm's way; or would slay the serpent.

13. EXPLOITS OF *WAN'-TAH*, MEDICINE MAN, AND THE *WAH'K-PUCH*[127]

Wan'-tah was a noted medicine man among the Yakimas, and was familiar with the ways and habits of the *wah'k-puch* [rattlesnake]. Gifted in their language, he conversed with them. He had power over the reptiles and made them subservient to his will. He was able to circumvent them in their most deadly machinations against the Indians.[128]

Um-toch, or *Um-touch*, a Klickitat residing on the lower Toppenish [creek], fell under the ban of the *wah'k-puch*. This, of course, was unknown to the intended victim, but *Wan'-tah*, through his *tah*, became aware of the plot. One day he came to his friend's house and acquainted him with the impending danger. A *wah'k-puch* was then lying in ambush for him. *Um-toch* was skeptical. He had not knowingly hurt or wronged one of the [rattlesnake] tribe, and could not understand such animosity against him. But *Wan'-tah* knew, and leading the way to a nearby pile of rails, soon uncovered a large rattler. The medicine man took the reptile in his hands, when it immediately became "like a walking stick," stiff and without the power to coil or strike.

Wan'-tah spoke to it: "Why are you here in hiding? Who sent you?"

The *wah'k-puch* replied: "I came to hunt the *cilk-cilk* [mice]. They are plenty here. I was hungry."

Wan'-tah retorted: "You speak lies! I know why you are here. You were sent by your [*wah'k-puch*] Chief to bite *Um-toch*, to kill him. I know what

I am going to do. I will fix you now. Any of your people following your trail will meet with the same fate. That fence is the line, the boundary. The *wah'k-puch* are not to cross to this side. Your Chiefs cannot delegate one of their men to do this evil thing against my people."

Wan'-tah then took an ax and chopped the rattler to pieces. This ended the plottings of the *wah'k-puch* against the life of *Um-toch* for all time. None have ever been known to pass beyond the "dead line" designated by the occult wisdom of the medicine man.

14. THE *WAH'K-PUCH* MIGRATES

The wild-grass meadow lands of the lower Reservation were formerly infested with the rattler during the summer months. Hibernating among the rocks of the Satus-Toppenish mountains, especially the *Ke-nute'*, or landslide[129] mentioned, they overran the meadows in quest of mice. With the introduction of the mowing machine, the reptiles were gradually exterminated.

In telling me of the former prevalence of the *wah'k-puch* and their subsequent disappearance from the prairie, an educated Indian said: "All about here the *wah'k-puch* were very numerous. On a sunny spring day, we could see them lying on the gravel, south side of our house.[130] They crawled from under the building, where they evidently wintered, to bask in the sun. We did not molest or kill them. None of us were ever bitten. When cutting hay, I would see the *wah'k-puch* writhe up and fall in pieces before the blades of the mower. Not once was my team bitten by them; but I did not like them. They are now all gone; left suddenly."

One day *Wan'-tah* came to my place and said: "You will no longer be bothered by the *wah'k-puch* on your ranch. I know what they are doing. The big horned Chief, living at the *Ke-nute'*,[131] has decided that his people are not to come here any more. He has sent his messenger, the swift, little brown *wah'k-puch*, to all the [rattlesnake] villages to warn his people not to travel over, or stay in the meadow lands."

"It is this way: Some of the *wah'k-puch* complained to their Chief that many of them had been killed where they had gone to the meadows to hunt *cilk-cilk* [mice]. Harming no one, they had been killed without warning. Why was this?"

"The Chief sent scouts to investigate, to learn about the trouble. The scouts returned and reported that it was something terrible that was killing them. *Ilquis* [wood] with hard parts, hard as their own stone houses.[132] They could not fight the monster; could not hurt it by biting it."

"The Chief sent other scouts who reported the same thing. They said: 'It is a terrible thing! It was standing still, and we examined it good without getting hurt. It has sharp teeth which move as does the lightning, biting the *wah'k-puch* to pieces. Our biting does not hurt it. No use trying to do anything. We cannot fight it; cannot stop it.'"

"Then the Chief counseled with his head men, and they decided to give up the grassy plains. He has ordered his people to stay away from the meadows. You need not be afraid of them. They will no longer bother you."

15. A STRANGE INCIDENT

The tribesman continued: "*Wan'-tah* could understand the language of the *wah'k-puch*, could hear them talking and laughing at a distance. I do not know how this was, but I know what I have seen with my own eyes. One day we were riding together on the trail, when *Wan'-tah* suddenly stopped and listened for a moment. I did not understand, but I also listened. I heard nothing.

"*Wan'-tah* turned to me and said: 'There are two *wah'k-puch* over there in the *to-mas'* bushes[133]. We will go see them.'

"The place he designated was beyond a swell in the ground, perhaps two hundred yards away. We could not see beyond this rise. We turned and rode over to the chokecherry bushes where we found two *wah'k-puch* lying together on the branches.

"*Wan'-tah* said that they were courting. We did not bother them. I do not know how *Wan'-tah* could tell that they were there. He said that he heard them talking."

16. EXPLOITS OF *WE-YAL-LUP WA-YA-CIKA*; A FATIGUED *WAH'K-PUCH* BEFRIENDED

That the *wah'k-puch* vacated the meadows in the way described by *Wan'-tah* is attested by other witnesses. An Indian policeman gave me the following incident as observed by himself.

He said: "The Indians were having a big roundup of horses not far from the Agency[134], and perhaps thirty miles from the landslide below Toppenish. A lot of Indians were sitting on the ground, gambling. Chief *We-yal-lup Wa-ya-cika* came to the camp and began to talk about the *wahk'-puch*.

"He said: 'The *wah'k-puch* are moving from their home along the mountain below Toppenish. They are coming up to the Soda Springs Canyon above here. They cannot fight the mowing machine killing them in the meadows. The horned Chief sent scouts to learn the cause of so many of his people being killed there, and they reported that it was a terrible *monster*, and that they could not stand in fight against it. That its teeth were swift and sharp, tearing them to pieces. The Chief has ordered his people to move. They are now on the trail."

One of the gamblers scoffed and said: "How do you know that the *wah'k-puch* are moving up to Soda Springs Canyon? Who has told you all this?"

We-yal-lup, the medicine man, did not like this talk. He retorted: "How do I know it? Have I not conversed with the *wah'k-puch* in council? Have I not talked to them on the trail? Today I came along the bluff-way. I found a *wah'k-puch* man lying near the burned place."

I said to him: "What are you doing here?"

He answered: "I am tired! I have traveled a long ways since the sunrise."

I then asked him: "Where are you going?"

He replied: "To Soda Springs Canyon. All *wah'k-puch* are going there."

I asked him why they were moving, and he told me the words I have already spoken. I took pity on the *wah'k-puch* man and said: "I am going a distance and will again cross the trail. I will take you with me and set you on the trail nearer the canyon."

The gambler, a young man who had gone to school, sneered as he shuffled his cards: "Listen to how he talks!"

The old medicine man drew from his coat-pocket a good-sized *wah'k-puch*, and casting it on the blanket among the gamblers exclaimed: "Here is my friend who I picked up on the trail! Ask him if my words are not true!"

There was a scattering among those card-players as the snake writhed into a coil and shook its warning rattles. No one now questioned the Chief's story. The medicine man recovered his pet with no seeming difficulty. Speaking to it softly in the Indian tongue, he took hold of it back of its head and replaced it in his pocket. We all saw this, and other Indians will tell you what I have told you.

17. A LURKING *WAH'K-PUCH*
FORESTALLED

The narrator[135] continued: "I kill the rattlesnake myself, for I was raised mostly among the white people. But there are strange things I do not understand. I was hunting with my cousin, and in camp one night he began singing his *tahmahnawis* song. He was asleep; sang for several minutes, then was silent. He did not wake up."

The next morning I asked why he sang, and he said: "I had a bad dream. Do not go ahead of me on the trail today when we approach the spring. A *wah'k-puch* is hiding there, waiting to bite someone. It is neither of us; but he might strike us, for he is awfully mad. Let me lead on the trail."

The spring he referred to was about fifteen miles away. We hunted till in the afternoon, and were returning to camp along the spring-trail. My cousin was in the lead; and when he reached the spring he got down from his horse and stepped to a bunch of small brush growing on the bank. He struck it with a stick and spoke: "What are you doing in there? I saw you last night, and I know why you are here. Come out from hiding! You cannot do this bad thing! I know why you hide along the trail!"

He was speaking low, and all the while reaching his hand under the brush. As he concluded his words, he drew out by its head a large rattlesnake. Catching it by either jaw, he tore it apart and threw it on the ground; a writhing, dying snake. I do not know how he knew the rattler was there; how he saw it. I only tell you what I heard in the night-song, and what I saw him do.[136]

18. A YOUNG WARRIOR *WAH'K-PUCH*[137]

Chief *We-yallup Wa-ya-cika*, medicine man, was riding with a friend across Ahtanum Mountain, on the 'Yal-lup Road.' Reaching the summit, the Chief reined in his horse and sat for a moment in an attitude of listening. Then turning abruptly aside he proceeded about fifty yards from the trail and dismounted at a tuft of wild sunflowers. To the amazement of his companion, he "poked" a small rattler from the withered leaves, addressing it as follows: "Why are you here? Hiding like a cowardly *Paiute* in the sage! I know your plans; what you intend doing! You cannot do that bad thing! I ought to kill you! But I will only rob you."

Then stripping the silk handkerchief from about his neck, he flaunted the bright-colored fabric in front of the belligerently coiled reptile. There was a lightning-like dart of the flattened head, when with a deft upward jerk of the handkerchief, the fangs were torn from the snake's mouth. Then, crushing the rattles on its tail, he again addressed it: "Now move along! You will do no harm for a time! You are a fine-looking warrior without your weapons; without your *power* rattle. Go! But the next time I find you in hiding for bad deeds, I will kill you! You know *'Yal-lup*! Who speaks not the lie."

The now harmless *wah'k-puch* crawled away in shame. Remounting, the medicine man explained to his mystified friend: "That was a young warrior *wah'k-puch*. He was on his first warpath. For three suns he had been hiding there, waiting to bite some Indian passing on the trail. He practiced jumping; leaping as if in fight. His war-song he sang while practicing the leap:

> This is the way I will
>   jump on the man!
> This is the way I will
>   kill my enemy!
> I am young! I am active.
> No one can escape my power."

"I heard his song last night as I slept. I saw him leaping from his hiding; saw him training for battle. He is not dangerous now. It will be many moons before his poison needles grow again."

19. CIRCUMVENTING A *WAH'K-PUCH*

A remarkable instance of the occult acumen of *We-yal-lup Wa-ya-cika*, Medicine Man, occurred only a short time before his death. The story is best told in the language of Simon Goudy, an intelligent half-blood, and as the one most deeply concerned. Mr. Goudy said: "I was up early that morning, when Chief *Yal-lup* rode into my barn corral, put his horse up, and fed it. He came to the house and we talked on different subjects. I did not ask him his business, but supposed that he wanted a team to do some plowing."

After breakfast, *Yal-lup* said: "Well, last night as I was sleeping in my old house, I heard the *tahmahnawis* song of a *wah'k-puch*. He sang of his work; what he intended doing. I saw the *wah'k-puch*. He had come down from *Mo-loc,* his home.[138] He wanted to cross to the Thap'panish, where he could find plenty of *cilk-cilk*. He came to the road just south of your house. There he saw where the wagons had passed; saw the wheel tracks. He heard the wagons rumbling on the road. He was afraid that he would be crushed and killed. He went back from that road a short distance and hid. He lay hid for a day, then tried to cross again. It was the same. Wagons passing all the time. For several days he tried to get across the road, but did not succeed. The wagons made him afraid."

Finally, the *wah'k-puch* thought: "It is this half-blood Injun who is doing this; who is killing us on the road. I am hungry! There is nothing here to eat. I will lay for this half-Injun. I will bite and kill him. I will get him out of the way of myself and my people."

I did not believe any of this, and so informed *Yal-lup*.

He said: "That *wah'k-puch* is now in hiding for you. Come! I will show you that my words are true."

Yal-lup led the way to the dry creek bed just outside the barn corral, at the base of *Pah-to-sah* [animal lying down].[139] He went straight to a tangled sagebrush, and striking it with a switch that he carried, he spoke, low but commandingly: "Come out! You are there! You know your old friend *Yal-lup*! I saw you last night in a dream! I heard your song! Come out!"

I was standing near. My wife was only a little ways from me, on the bank. I saw a big rattlesnake crawl from that brush; come out on the side next to *Yal-lup*. I felt my hair tingle; going on end. My wife was badly scared! She saw that snake, same as I. *Yal-lup* struck it with the switch; not too hard, but enough to smart and sting.

He spoke to the snake: "Now move along! Get back to *Mo-loc*, your home. I ought to kill you, but will let you go this time. Keep traveling! Do not stop till you are at your own house."

That rattler did not fight the switch. It just kept moving. It crawled away, going towards *Mo-loc*. It continued in that direction as far as I could see. No! I was not afraid that it might not go back to the big rock.

I was not afraid that it would stay at my place. No! *Yal-lup* could not have placed the snake under that sagebrush. I saw him ride in and dismount. I saw him come to the house. He did not go near where the rattler was hiding. It was more than an hour after he came before he mentioned about the snake. I do not know how he knew that it was there. I only know what he told me, and what I saw with my own eyes. I do not try to account for the old man's wisdom. I only know that he can hear and see things far beyond my understanding.

20. MORE EXPLOITS OF *WE-YAL-LUP WA-YA-CIKA*; STORIES OF THE *WAH'K-PUCH*

Some day I will tell you about the *wah'k-puch*. The little one; not the big Chief with horns.[140] I am now the only living Yakima who knows about the *wah'k-puch*, who understands their language. I will tell you, but to none other. You are my best friend, but I must have pay for my talk.[141] It is valuable; I cannot give it away.

The white man has telegraph wires by which he sends messages to distant places. The *wah'k-puch* has a way of communication without that. If he loses a son or daughter, he immediately knows it; can inform his remotest people. Whites cannot understand these things. Not all Indians understand at this day. In former times Indians possessed more power than now. Changes have come to my people.

A company of *wah'k-puch* live at the big rock at *Pah'-qy-ti-koot*. That rock stands on the bank of the *Ahtanum*, just above the Gap. That rock makes the cold wind to blow through the Gap. Its name is *Tho'-wit-tet* [cold wind]. A horned Chief *wah'k-puch* was there.

I was bitten twice by the *wah'k-puch*. Once on the thumb; once on the foot. I drank about a bucket of water and then ran. You could not catch me. I was crazy, wild. I will tell you sometime how I was bitten; how I cured myself. I will tell you how I cured others bitten by the *wah'k-puch*. The time is not good to speak of it now.

There was once a big animal, a monster seen on the bluff at Zillah [the Washington town] on the Yakima River. In the long ago it lived in the water. It died there on the bluff where in after years its bones could be seen. I will tell you about it when I talk of the *wah'k-puch*.[142]

21. BOY BITTEN BY A *WAH'K-PUCH*[143]

I promised you a story of the *wah'k-puch*. Not the big one with the horns and with war paint across his forehead, but the little one that you see.

When Erwin was our agent, Dr. Willgus was the Reservation doctor. One morning in August, Henry *Wee-ah-neen-tla*, a little boy in the Agency school, was bitten by a *wah'k-puch*, one of good size. All day Dr. Willgus could not help the child. About sundown, Charley *Selister* came for me. They would give me a good gray work horse and a new saddle if I go cure the boy. Not many saddles here then. I wanted that saddle.

I thought: "Yes! I will cure the boy for the

horse and saddle. They are mine now." It was late and
I said to *Selister*: "I cannot go tonight. It is too late.
Let the boy die. If his life is still living in the morning,
I will bring him back again."[144]

I staked my saddle horse and slept. About two
o'clock [A.M.] I started. I arrived at the Agency about
sunrise. They said to me: "Boy still alive, but nearly
gone."

I found Charles Mann there.[145] Dr. Willgus
would not let visitors see the boy. Father of the child
was about crying. He told me: "Doctor will not let you
see him."

They said to the Doctor and the Agent: "*Yal-
lup* has come to cure the child."

I went upstairs where the boy lay. Dr. Willgus
and Erwin the Agent came. Erwin said to me: "You
Indians lie! You cannot doctor."

Charles Mann spoke to me in our own tongue:
"Make up your strong mind to cure the boy. If you
cannot cure him, say so."

I had not seen the horse and saddle. I came to
the boy. He was in bed; breath nearly out. Fingers and
arm puffed big; bit in thumb. Lots of bottles with
white doctor's medicine. I felt the boy's shoulder.
Poison is there. Shirt sleeve all torn; arm big as your
leg. The white doctor *iyix* [sat] here, Agent there, one
on each side of the bed.

I held the shoulder; poison needles there. Arm
bandaged tight, but poison got through. When Mann
said to me: "Only make one mind to cure him!"

I did so. I pressed my hands on both sides of
swollen arm like this [stroking slowly down the arm to
affected thumb]! Poison is like water. It leaked out. I

only took out part of poison; let some remain a short time.

I went out to the horse given me. The boy's mother said: "You cured him now? Cured him entirely?"

I saw the horse. I do not like the horse. I see the saddle. I do not like the saddle. It is secondhand. If I knew the kind of pay, I would not cure the boy; I let him go. If I knew this, I would not come to cure him.

Charles Mann said: "Now my brother-in-law![146] Do not feel bad! They will exchange the horse."

I will stay outside, outdoors. Then I thought: "I will finish up! I will cure the child!"

Then I take out my pipe, tobacco, and smoke. Many Indians, some whites there to see me. While I smoke, black clouds come fast over the mountain woods. I finish smoke. When I finish smoke, big hail falls from above, from the clouds. My *power* was in the hail.[147] Dr. Willgus and Agent do not believe in Indian *power*. White people cannot understand our ways.

Then I went back to the little boy. I worked the thumb and let the poison out. In about half an hour, I am going home. Before starting, I said to the parents: "You take the boy home now."

They make reply: "If he die on the way?"

I answered: "Never mind! Take him home. Do not hear the white doctor."

They took the child home, and he got well. He is still living; strong, grown man. They exchanged the horse; gave me a better horse.

22. BITTEN WHILE PURLOINING
VEGETABLES

I will tell you two other stories. I, *We-yal-lup Wa-ya-cika*, was twice bitten by the *wah'k-puch*. I got ashamed! I was stealing in the *Qy-yi-ches*. Injuns had peas in garden. Two of us went over there. We went into garden; Injuns all gone to mountains. Nobody there. Peas all dry. We ate them. I was in corner where there was shade. *Wah'k-puch* there. It did not sound tail-rattle. It jumped, bit me on [great] toe. Bit through moccasin.

I said to my companion: "I get bit!"

Wah'k-puch run off. We chased him; killed him. We went on.

My partner said: "You going to die!"

This was long snows ago. Nobody knew I was doctor. I said: "Never mind! I will not die." I let the poison come up on me. We rode on to the *Titon* [Tieton] River. My heart feels badly. It is very little. I am going to die.

Then I make myself strong with my *power*. I took my leg like this [encompassing the limb with both hands, compressing slowly to end of the great toe]! I drive the poison down, take it way. It leaks like water. I am cured.

23. BITTEN ON THE TRAIL

I was in the *Titon* [Tieton] Basin building fish traps. Four of us went on the river trail to spear salmon. We saw the *wah'k-puch* on the trail ahead of us. It went in the black sage [greasewood]. I went to feel for that snake. I could not find him. Then I saw him under the bush. I took stick and squeeze down on his head. I held him fast. Then I caught him by the neck like this [thumb and forefinger]. I held his mouth next [pointing] to me. That *Wah'k-puch* wrapped around my arm. The Injuns watching me. Snake is tied tight around my arm. He is big; is strong. I nearly let him go.

Injuns tell me: "Let him alone! You get bit!"

I took stick to beat his head, want to scare him. I said to him: "What in hell you travel on trail for? Injun trail! You must not go on trail! Keep away!"

I hit the *wah'k-puch* twice. He swung around and bit me here [base of thumb]. Then I beat his head hard, killed him. I threw him among the brush, leave him there. I go about quarter mile. I feel the poison.

I said to my friends: "I am bit!"

Two Injuns stayed behind, other one came on with me. We spear two salmon. I feel my heart like a little finger. I will die!

I said: "I am poisoned! Let me go home." I run fast. I am crazy. You cannot catch me; go like racehorse.

I get to camp and say to my wife: "I am bit by *wah'k-puch*. Give me water." She gets bucket of water; I drink all. I am dry.

I say: "Get more! This not enough!" She brings another bucket full. I drink it all.

I then tell my wife: "I am poisoned! I will die!"

She said to me: "Do not be ashamed! Do not say you will die!"

I lay down on the blankets. I hold my thumb tight. I recovered. I said to my wife: "Do not be afraid!

I will not die!" I took the poison out by the finger. I took it all away.[148]

24. CHALLENGE OF THE MEDICINE MAN

I will tell how our Agent acted with the Injun doctors. General Milroy was Agent. He said: "You Injuns are liars! You are no doctors. White men are doctors. Only one doctor here at Agency. You Injun doctors will all die."

Injuns all feel bad. Injun doctors all to be killed [displaced] by the Agency Doctor. The old people said: "No! We will not live behind, will not doctor with the white man."

The Agent said: "Your Injun ways will die!" This hurt the Injuns. They want a big council: Catholics, Methodists, *Pom-poms*, Medicine Dancers. All agree about what the Agent said. Agent wants to kill Injun doctoring.

The Agent appointed a day for big council. Built stand outside at Fort [Simcoe] with seats all around. Injuns come from every part of Reservation. Injun doctors all there. Agent stood up and spoke: "You must quit these Injun doctors! They are no good! There is only one doctor now, this white doctor."

The big, old Injun doctors all get scared at Agent's words. These doctors are all dead now.

The Agent grew brave. He said: "If you have strong, bad spirit, kill me! Kill dog! If you cannot kill dog, you are no doctors."

He then offered one hundred dollars to reward the Injun doctor who could kill him. *Antrim*, the *Chi-*

mookle [Negro] Interpreter, offered another hundred dollars, same as Agent.

Injun doctors do not talk; all scared. All are afraid of Agent. I got mad! I was no doctor.[149] My *power* was in middle of my heart. I stood up and talked. I was ashamed of the Injun doctors. I said: "I hear your talk. They are big words! I never make lies about Injun doctors. I know *power* exists among all the tribes.

"You have white children. You send them to school to learn trades. They are taught to lecture; doctor; lawyer; carpenter; blacksmith or other trades. One learns one thing, some learn others. This is the white man's way. Injun way is different."

"My father, mother, brother, sister, cousins, nephews, uncles and aunts all have different ways from yours. I will tell you: When I was a little boy, my uncle whipped me to make me go to mountain. No! I would not go. Then he whipped me. Worst whipping I ever get. I cry like a dog; howl like a dog and go off where he tells me. You go there, stay one night; three nights. Maybe five nights. I went to find *power* to be doctor; or to be brave to go to war. *Power* to go sly; steal horses from the enemy and not be found. *Power* to hunt the *yah'-mas*, the bear, the mountain goat. *Power* to catch the salmon, the sturgeon or other fish. I found *power* to be a doctor. Have you *power*? Let us see your *power*!"

The Agent did not show us his *power*, did not tell us about any of his *power*.

Then I said to Millroy and his interpreter: "I will steal your two hundred dollars now. What is your *power*? I got *power* from the *wah'k-puch*. If you have power, we will see which is strongest. I will get *wah'k-puch*, let him bite you on each side of your mouth. I will let you nearly die. Then I will bring you back to life and save you. I will have no medicine in bottles like white doctor. I have spoken enough."

Chief *White Swan* touched Millroy on leg and said: "Never mind him! You better not do this. He is a powerful man! All the Injuns know him."

Millroy then said to the Injuns: "If you get the Injun doctor and die, you will not get what you pay returned. The doctor is to keep it all." The Injun doctors said: "No! We do not want it that way. We do not steal! We will give it all back."

We are still here, Injun doctors. Agent let us go. We held council, and some agree to pay back half if sick people die. But some pay back all. I never take pay if they die.

25. POTENCY OF A MEDICINE MAN'S POWER

In a talkative mood, the medicine man[150] volunteered: "If **woman** *wah'k-puch* gets mad at you, if she bites you, I do not think I can cure you. But if **man** *wah'k-puch* bites you, I can cure. I have doctor power to cure man poison. I get this *power* when a little fellow. I can not get it when big. My *power* is valuable. It is worth about twenty-five million dollars [sic.]. When Injun gets sick, they send for me. I go and cure."

I say: "My *power* for cash!" Then I find out how much they will pay. How many horses; how many cattle; blankets or money. If you are there, you can write it and take photographs. Make it into history.

If Injun dies, I return all pay. This is way of old Injun doctor. White doctor charges by the mile. They do not give back money if you die. They keep all. I do not do this. It is just like stealing.

If you are bit by *wah'k-puch*, I return all to your family. Some Injun doctors do not do this. Like White doctors they keep all. Others keep one half. This is not good. The Agent spoiled them.

This is all I will tell you today. This ends for this day. All I tell is true. I do not tell the lie. I might go [to] the bad adobe (?) where the sun sets. I am bad enough without lying.

26. DEATH OF A MEDICINE MAN[151],[152]

Chief *We-yal-lup Wa-ya-cika* was a good man and presiding Indian judge of the Indian Court on the Yakima Reservation. He was noted as a good man and also as a good Indian doctor among his Tribes. He has cured many by his practice of *power*. When at last he came to his death, it was [the result/cause of] his *power* while doctoring.

[While doctoring] at Wapato [modern town on Yakima Reservation], he got a *power* out of a patient, but this *power* overpowered his *power* with which he had cured many. George Meninock and his wife he cured one time, who are living today, and many others.

When at last he came to his death bed, he confessed that he had gotten out a *power*, a bad spirit from a sick girl whose bad spirit had then overpowered his *power*, and killed him. Nothing could cure him.

White men do not believe that the Indian man's power comes out of rocks and trees and animals and water. But when with the deluge of water god once drowned this earth, the wicked people all drowned, died in that flood. Their souls went into this earth, into rocks, animals, snakes, trees, and water through the Devil and settled among the Indian tribes all over the world which exists now, this day.[153]

Among Indians only the *power* of the Devil persists, and this is true as when a young Indian boy's parents used to whip him and make him hunt such power up in the mountains. [With] nothing to eat for five nights or more, and when a young feller, he found such a bad power from a rock, from a tree, from water, or from the animal. It talked to him and gave him power. This is out of a Devil which exists in this earth.

And when a young brave found a power to be a fighter, he was a fighter [warrior] with arrows and gun when his white brother brought the guns in this country. Now we have heard the story told in wars where one or two braves defeated soldiers such as Custer's fight and his death, and [Chief] Joseph's flight, and how it was done.

It was through a [man's] power out of a Devil being [through] in a stone or a whist [?]. And now the red man is getting to civilization [becoming civilized] and is training his children this way. All are sending their children to school to learn of white man's power, by and by to be successful men and women, and to learn the bad. Some will turn out to be grafters, etc. This is white man's power today—only rich people are good in law but [are] hell with a poor white man. Just the same an Indian rich man wants more by [through] a graft, but the time is coming, slow and sure, [and] he will die just the same as a poor man, [go to hell because of his riches]. As a matter of fact, evil rests in monies. This is a white man's power. When time ends in this earth, we shall be in a same spirit and soul. And when we are bad while living in this earth, we will go to see the devil. This is no josh [joke] of Mr. Bad Injun [in his letters Louis Mann often refers to himself as a "bad injun"] written for a story.

Mrs. Caesar Williams (*Yes-to-lah-lemy*) was the source for Death Journey Visions from both her mother and her father, nos. 50 and 60 hereafter. Historical Photograph Collections, Washington State University Libraries.

An-a-whoa (Black Bear), d. Aug 1918. With her husband, *Quas-qui Taichens*, a narrator of death journey visions. Historical Photograph Collections, Washington State University Libraries.

I-keeps-swah (Sitting Rock) ["Wasco Jim"], 1918. Historical Photograph Collections, Washington State University Libraries.

CHAPTER FIVE

REMARKABLE ACCOUNTS
OF SHAMANS' *TAHMAHNAWIS* POWERS

This chapter catalogs briefly some of the variety of *tahmahnawis* spirits which were acquired by the Yakima shaman. Indeed, spirit power might be obtained from animals, birds, snakes, fish, and natural phenomena as well as water, rocks, clouds, thunder and lightning. We have already noted that *tah* power was obtained from dwarfs, also ghosts. But this chapter notes still other *tahmahnawis* sources. First, spirit power was acquired not only from fish and animals of rivers and streams, but also from the "water people," men as well as women beings for whom *Nash-lah'* was chief, and who bestowed spirit power on certain individuals.[154] Second, spirit powers from dried fish or deer bones provided protection against great danger for their owners. They were the source of protective *tah* for warriors so that they could not be killed in battle. Third, some animals or birds such as the owl gave *tahmahnawis* to some hunters enabling them to locate the precise whereabouts of game.

Another *tah* gave some the power to locate lost graves of the dead that they might be reblanketed, then reburied. Oftentimes, a shaman's prophetic dreams portended the fate an individual might meet the next day. But some *tahs* which might come to the shaman were malevolent and thus uncontrollable, spirit powers of dread and evil. At least one narrative cites that such malevolent *tahs* came of the spirit powers from the white horse, and the buffalo bull.

A. AQUATIC *TAHS*

27. *WAN'-TAH'S* ADVENTURE WITH THE *WAL-CHI-O*[155]

Wan'-tah was the maternal grandfather of my [L.V. McWhorter's] narrator, and often told his grandchild the particulars of his singular adventure. The soldiers at Fort Simcoe called him *Wan'-to*, and in time he was known among the Indians by that name. A Dalles Indian [Wasco?][Wishram?], he lived at that place when the occurrence happened.

With two other tribesmen, *Wan'-tah* was crossing the *n-Che'-wana* above the rapids, when the canoe capsized and all were thrown into the stream. His companions managed to reach shore, but *Wan'-tah* was carried over the *Tum-wah-ter*, or falls. As he went down with the cataract, he called to his *tahmahnawis*: "I am going to die!"

Wan'-tah was caught in the boiling undertow and swirled round and around, until life was almost beaten out of him. But his *tahmahnawis* had not forsaken him. On the verge of unconsciousness, he felt his head shoot from the water and his body strike a rocky shore. Dazed, he lay for a short time recovering his breath, and then pulled himself forward out of the water. *Wan'-tah* then knew that he was not going to die.

Although breathing the air of the outer world, *Wan'-tah* found himself in the blackest darkness. It was morning when he had been thrown into the flood, but here he could see no sun, no sky, no moon nor stars. He could hear nothing but the muffled murmur of rushing water, and its low, musical lap on a pebbly shore. He was in an underground chamber of some kind, but what? Was it a subterranean cavern, inhabited by the *water-people* of the *n-Che'-wana*? Or was it the dwelling place of the people-devouring *Ishi-tah plah*? Helpless, the young Indian could only await developments.

By and by *Wan'-tah* detected a slight noise at the edge of the lapping water. It was as of some creature coming ashore. He heard a distinct breathing, and a soft flapping and scraping on the smooth stones. This was followed by another, and still another. Soon his naked leg was brushed by a moving wet body. He shifted position, and came in contact with others. The deep breathing, now on every side, filled the place, and was rapidly augmented by accessions to the invisible intruders. They swarmed up from the watery darkness. *Wan'-tah* could no longer avoid his uncanny visitors, had he so attempted. The cavern was permeated with a rank, fishy smell.

Summoning his *tah* powers, *Wan'-tah* cautiously felt about and discovered that he was in the midst of a herd of the *wal-chi-o*; the river, or freshwater seal. He then knew that it was nightfall, and that the *wal-chi-o* had left off fishing in the boil of the *Tum-wah-ter*, until the next sunrise. He was in the great sleeping lodge of the *wal-chi-o*. Soon the uneasy shuffling on the rock-floor ceased, and the deeper

respiration told the young warrior that the *wal-chi-o*
were sleeping—sleeping with intervals of starting
wakefulness—an inherent trait of this alert little animal.

Wan'-tah now conceived a desperate plan of
escape. Moving slowly and with caution among the
slumbering hosts, he groped until he found the largest,
the Chief of all the *wal-chi-o*. He well knew the habits
of the river-seal. It would sleep during the night and
at the earliest dawn sally forth in quest of salmon. It
was *Wan'-tah's* intention to grasp and hold onto the
big Chief when he should dive into the water, well
knowing that he would immediately rise to the surface
for air. The Indian thus hoped to be carried beyond the
deadly grip of the *Tum-wah-ter*, where swimming to
shore would be an easy task. With this determination
matured, *Wan'-tah* lay down by the Chief and slept.

Wan'-tah was at all times a light sleeper, and
now his unusual surroundings augmented this trait of
the hunter and warrior. Often he awoke, sat up and
listened to the drowsy sounds about him. The odor
was decidedly "fishy," but the breath of the *wal-chi-o*
in a measure tempered the chilly dampness of the
cavern to such extent that he suffered no great
inconvenience from cold.

After seemingly an incredibly long period,
Wan'-tah heard a sharp: "*Chic-chic!*" which was
immediately answered by a like chorus throughout the
spacious cavern. It was the call of the Chief. The *wal-
chi-o* well knew the best fishing hour, and hastened to
plunge into the water. The supreme moment had
arrived.

Wan'-tah had slept with one hand lightly
touching the Chief, and as he felt him stirring, he was

careful not to let him pass beyond his reach. Life and death stood side and side in that cavernous blackness. The young Indian was now singing his "medicine" song, given him by his guardian *tah*. As the Chief surged into the black waves, *Wan'-tah* threw himself upon his back, encircling the body with his arms and grasping firmly the base of each flipper. Down and out from that cavern's mouth dived the frightened Chief, out into the death-churn of the dreaded *Tum-wah-ter*. Up through that maelstrom of terror shot the mighty swimmer with such force that the lithe Indian could scarce retain his precarious and slippery hold. The *Tum-wah-ter* tore like spirit-giants at his hands, and dragged as stone at his feet. Shooting sparks flashed before his strained vision, and rumbling detonations like that of the mountain avalanche filled his bursting ears. Confused murmurings, followed a semi-consciousness—a floating through space—then the soft morning light bursting in his face. *Wan-tah* found himself on the bosom of the blue rolling *n-Che'-wana*, safely below the boiling tow of the *Tum-wah-ter*. Swimming ashore, he rested for a time on the rocky beach; then walked to the village.

As *Wan'-tah* approached his own tepee, he heard the women wailing for the dead. Lifting the door-flap, he entered. His wife, *Noh-a-tehs* had cut her long hair in accordance with the tribal custom of bereavement; and with relatives was giving vent to lamentations of grief.

Wan'-tah spoke: "*Noh-a-tehs*! Why is this? Who is *at-nan-na* [dead]?"

Noh-a-tehs looked up startled. She saw her husband standing before her, alive. She said: "You went down in the pouring *Tum-wah-ter*. You did not come back. All day, all night have I cried because you were *at-nan-na*. How have you come from the *n-Che'-wana*?"

Wan'-tah heard his wife and said: "No! I did not *at-nat* [die] in the *Tum-wah-ter*. My medicine was good! I slept in the rock-lodge of the *wal-chi-o*. The Chief brought me through the death-water. I swam ashore; I am here. Where the sun is now, my name shall be *Yah-ti tah-nee*; for I have come back from the water."

28. AQUATIC TAHMAHNAWIS[156]

A. *Al'-o-tut* possessed a *tah* obtained from some aquatic animal, which enabled him without apparent injury to remain under water an unusual length of time. Once he was thrown into the *tumwater* of the *n-Che'-wana* where rescue by his companions was impossible. He was caught in the "churn" of the falls, where logs and other drift are ofttimes held until released by the annual floods. Although an expert swimmer, *Al'-o-tut* was helpless in combatting the reflex of the falls. Great sturgeons disported in the midst of this deadly swirl, and *Al'-o-tut* conceived a novel though desperate mode of escape. Calling upon his *tah*, he seized hold of a large sturgeon, grasping tight to its fins. Frightened, the mighty fish dashed away at terrific speed. Its course led down stream with the current which enabled *Al'-o-tut* to retain his hold until carried beyond the return drag of the falls; where he easily regained the shore. *Al'-o-tut* was known along other lines of accomplishments. He died about 1900.

B. Another tribesman still living is reputed to possess a *tah* similar to that of *Al'-o-tut*. At one time he walked down the sloping bed of a river beyond his depth where, seated on a boulder [under the water?], he drew a small flask of whiskey from his pocket. Drinking the contents, he recorked the bottle and let it float to the surface. He then came ashore rejoining his companions in camp. At another time as a joke on his hungry associates, he seized an only fish baking at the fire, sprang beneath the surface of the stream and there devoured it. He is also said to have entered Lake Chelan, exploring considerable of its uneven bed. When asked about these accomplishments, the hero laughed and said: "No Injun do that! No Injun stay in water more than one breath."

C. *Antwine*, a noted medicine man living in the Kittitas Valley [perhaps the general vicinity of Ellensburg, WA], obtained his *tah* in the following manner: Years ago his brother went over the tumwater in a canoe and was lost. He did not drown as supposed, but was caught by a woman of the water people, and taken to her underwater home. He married this woman and lived with her for a time. While the river envelops these habitations, the dwellings are dry and comfortable.

Antwine was *tah*-seeking, and while in a trance was conveyed by his lost brother to his subterranean abode. There the water people gave him the power of healing along certain lines. He can extract pins, splinters of wood or other foreign substances from any part of the human body, without pain to the patient. One case was that of a woman suffering with a broken needle completely imbedded in her hand. Two white surgeons had failed in giving relief, suggesting an operation as the only remedy. *Antwine* painlessly removed the corroding steel within a few minutes.

D. Many years ago a *Wasco* man was supposedly drowned in the *n-Che'-wana* at *Tenino*. Several days after his disappearance he was seen sitting with a woman on an island a little above where the town of Tenino now stands [in 1911?]. The man was fully recognized by his people. The woman was hunting the lice on his head. She was a fine-looking woman, with hair falling about her person in great billowy waves. The Wasco afterwards returned home and did not go back to the Water People. He had been caught by *Nash-lah'*, Chief of the Water People, who married him to his daughter.[157]

29. CHIEF SLUSKIN'S *TAHMAHNAWIS*[158]

When a boy, Sluskin saw (in a vision) a woman coming from the far east [from the Bitteroot Range?]. A baby was born to her on the lower Yakima [River? valley?]. She came on up the river and talked to Sluskin and gave him the *tahmahnawis* of Lake Kachess,[159] the source of the Yakima River. Thus it was that he could at certain times eat to surfeiting and experience no inconvenience. On such occasions he was feeding his *tahmahnawis*, the lake, not himself.

Once Sluskin was hunting horses on the desert plain around where Toppenish now stands, and slept

overnight amid the sage brush. Next morning he went
to an Indian camp on the river somewhere opposite
(now) Toppenish, where they had a fish trap. All the
Indians were absent but one woman. Sluskin inquired
if she had seen his horses and was answered in the
negative. He then asked her for a bite to eat.

Complying, the woman built a fire, put on a
large kettle filled with salmon to boil, and began
baking bread, such as is so commonly made in the
Indian camps, consisting of cakes baked in a well-
greased frying pan, turned or "flipped," and known as
"bannocks." In the meantime a large boiler of coffee
was placed on the coals to brew. The "bannocks"
began to stack up, and Sluskin thought: "This poor
woman is feeling sorry for me, thinks I am very
hungry, and wants to feed me. I do not want her to get
so tired cooking for me. I only wanted a small bite to
eat."

Then he said to her: "Do not work and cook so
much, do not make yourself tired. Give me just a small
piece of something to eat, so I will not get so hungry."

"I will feed you," was her reply as she continued
stacking up the "bannocks."

This touched Sluskin's pride. He was offended.
He answered mentally to himself: "All right! She
wants to feed me—I will eat."

He sat watching her bake "bannocks" until a
stack nearly two feet high was completed. Then she
went to the garden, or truck patch, and brought in a
gunnysack of watermelons. These she cut in slices, set
out the salmon and "bannocks," poured coffee, and
bade him eat.

Sluskin thought: "This poor woman has tired

herself to feed me. I will eat."

Seating himself on the ground by the spread, he began the feast. Draining his cup of coffee, he called for more. Salmon and "bannocks" began to disappear rapidly. Soon the coffee was all gone. Another boiler was placed to boil, while Sluskin continued paying his respects to salmon and "bannocks." The coffee done, it was not long until the boiler was again emptied and placed for the third brewing. Salmon and "bannocks" were getting low.

The third boiler of coffee was ready and Sluskin asked: "Where is sugar?"

"No more sugar."

"No more sugar? Why do you keep so little sugar. You do not have much to give me."

The boiler was soon emptied despite the dearth of sugar, and the salmon and "bannocks" nearly exhausted.

"More coffee! Where is coffee?"

"No more coffee."

"You do not have much. Well, I must eat without coffee."

"'Bannocks' all gone," Sluskin said. "No Bread? Where is bread?"

The woman baked more "bannocks," baked until her stock of flour was exhausted, a 50-pound bag.

Sluskin called: "Where is bread? I see no bread!"

"Flour all gone."

"No more flour? You do not keep much flour."

By this time the salmon had all disappeared and Sluskin spoke: "Where is salmon? You did not cook much salmon."

"No more salmon."

"No more salmon? You do not have much salmon. Here is dried salmon."

"You can eat; you can get the salmon," was the reply.

"All right! I will eat. I feed my *tahmahnawis* now."

Reaching up, Sluskin pulled down piece after piece of dried salmon where it hung overhead, stripping out the bones and eating. Soon the supply was exhausted.

"Where is salmon? I do not see any here."

"No more salmon."

"No more salmon? You do not have much salmon. Well, I must eat roots. I feed my *tahmahnawis* now."

He hauled the baskets of dried roots from storage and continued eating. Soon the supply was exhausted and Sluskin again spoke: "Where are roots? You do not have many roots."

"No more roots!"

"All right. You do not have much to eat. I will take melon now."

It was not long until the melons were cleaned up and again came the repeated call for more food. "Where are melons? I like melons. You do not give me many!"

"You can get them from the patch, if you want more," was the reply.

Sluskin retorted: "You do not give me much to eat. You tell me: 'No more!' I will have to get melons myself. I am feeding my *tahmahnawis* now."

Going out to the melon patch, he cleaned up

the last of them and then rode away.

The men returning to camp found every vestige of food gone, nothing with which to allay their own pangs of hunger. They chided the woman for what she had done, telling her that she should not have tried to feed him, only given him a small breakfast. It was useless, they said, to attempt to feed Sluskin's *tahmahnawis*.

Sluskin often told his friends not to try "feeding" him, but always give him just a little food, same as anyone else. Then he would not invoke his *tahmahnawis* power, which could not be satiated.

Sluskin was helping some of his friends with their haying on the Ahtanum [Ridge vicinity?]. It was a hot day and all went to the well for water. Sluskin took the cup and drained it the third time, when one of the young men jokingly said: "There is the barrel [bucket]. It is best for you. You cannot drink it full."

Sluskin accepted the challenge: "You put up ten dollars that I can not drink five barrels [buckets]? I take your money sure."

The young man would not bet. Sluskin then said: "I will drink. I will drink, for I am dry."

He drained the bucket and, letting it down, brought it up full. It was drained again, and again brought up and poised on the curb.

Alarmed, the young man remonstrated, saying that it would kill him. Sluskin paid no attention, but drank the bucket dry. The fourth time the bucket came up and, despite the protest of those watching him, he emptied it and brought it up for the fifth time.

The protests were now more urgent. The Indians believed him crazy and expected to see him drop over dead.

But no! The fifth and last bucket of water was swallowed without any apparent or visible effect on the drinker who smilingly said: "I quit now. Five times drinking was what I told you. I will not drink more than that. I have spoken the truth; five barrels [buckets] only do I drink this time."

PROTECTIVE TAHS[160]

30. YAKIMA *TAHMAHNAWIS* POWER: THE BOY AND THE BRAVE HAZEL NUT[161]

There was among the Yakimas a noted warrior whose skill and prowess in battle was unequaled among his own, or surrounding tribes. Though often surrounded and seized by the enemy, he was always able to break away from them and elude pursuit. His secretive power was unsurpassed. No number of the enemy could overcome or hold him secure. This mysterious power lay in the following incident.

A man was cracking hazel nuts on a large stone, using a smaller stone as a hammer. He struck one of the nuts an ordinary blow, when it sprang from his grasp, lighting some distance away. He picked it up and again attempted to smash it with his hammer stone, when it escaped the second time.

The man said to it: "You are brave, but I will break you anyhow." He then seized it more firmly and dealt it a heavier blow. It leaped into the grass, where the most diligent search failed to reveal its hiding place, although the sharp-eyed Indian saw where it had disappeared.

Afterwards a small boy in search of his *tahmahnawis* came upon the hazel nut in hiding, and it spoke to him: "Look at me, my boy! And listen to what I am telling you. The enemy cannot hold me nor hurt me, although I am struck heavy blows. I hide and none can find me. I am strong. I will give you my strength; and if you will do as I tell you, you will possess my power. The enemy may surround you and catch you; they cannot hold you. You can spring from their grasp and hide before their eyes and they cannot find you."

The young Indian followed faithfully the secret rulings laid down by the voice from the hazel nut, and he ever [since has] had the mysterious power of escaping and hiding from his enemies. He became the renowned warrior spoken of.

31. THE SOURCE OF *HISTO'S* POWER AS A WARRIOR[162],[163]

McWhorter to the Interpreter: "Histo has been a great warrior and gone through many dangers in battle and on the trail. He must have had some power, other than that given him by his father, as he told me last year when narrating his Modoc War story.[164] Tell him what I have said, and ask him about his secret power—what it can be."

Interpreter repeated, and *Histo* solemnly replied: "When I was small, my mother left me near the water. I heard the wind in the firs, and I could see the tops and branches of the trees moving.

"The wind passed through the trees, but the trees were not hurt. The trees talked to me. They said: 'Look at us, little boy. You can see us shaken and hear the wind passing through us, but we are not hurt. The wind cannot hurt us. We will give you our power. You do as we tell you, and you will be like us. Nothing will hurt you. The arrows and bullets of the enemy will pass you, but you will not be hurt.'

"The first then gave me rules to go by. I followed the instructions, and I have had the power of the firs. Nothing could hurt me in battle."

After delivering this speech, *Histo* added with some degree of regret: "Now I have told you how I got my power, and it has left me. I am just like a sheep that is to have its head cut off. I cannot help myself. I have told you my power, how I got it, and it has gone from me.[165] I am no longer any good."

32. *HISTO'S* NARRATIVE OF HIS FATHER[166],[167]

I was telling you a story of when I was young, when the Bannocks came and killed people and carried all my playmates away. I will tell you another story. It was when I was young that my father went on the warpath. Many went, a few only remained at home. They went farther than the Modoc country. They traveled through, and around there. Two men separated from the band. One was my father. They stopped over and then traveled the next day, and found one tepee. The man with my father was a strong, brave warrior.

My father was also a strong man and a brave man. They smoked and talked about how to capture the tepee.

The man of the tepee found out that they were around, and he left with his wife. They had a fight. He fought the two. They never killed him. He got the little pappose and hung it on the horn of his saddle.

The two men had [a] muzzle loading gun, one that used caps. The man with my father spilled the caps. He said: "Well! Let's go home." They led their horses and walked.

The man of the tepee followed them and shot nine arrows into my father, all over from behind. The other man was not touched. This man's power was from the eel.

He said to his power: "What is the use of being this way? I would like to be hit one time anyway."

After this, he turned around, facing the enemy close. The tepee man shot him in the eye with an arrow. The arrow seemed to wobble and quiver the same as if shot into a tree.

He thought: "I am shot once." The tepee man shot no more.

The man said to my father: "I do not like this arrow in my eye. Pull it out."

Father went up to him, but only broke it off.

My father said: "You pull the arrows from me, from behind."

The man did the same thing that my father had done. He broke the arrows off. They did not try to pull them out.

They traveled on. One horse, shot in the leg, swelled up. The arrows were poisoned with rattlesnake poison. They went on.

My father said: "I am getting weak. Leave me here and go home with my horse in a hurry. Tell them to come after me. If I am dead, cut me in two and carry me home in two pieces." The horse shot in the leg was no good.

They stretched [a] rawhide rope across the trail, so they could find my father in the night. The man rode away and went fast. My father lay all day and all night. It was very hot, in July. He had no water and nearly starved for water. He made water in his hand and wet his throat.

At last the people came to him and said: "You still alive? We thought you would be dead by this time. We think that you have some strong power, [that] is reason you are alive. It is bothering us lots. Tell us about your power and get more power in you."

He then told of his power. The place is called *Chlu-qui-tum*, above Celilo, Oregon. A hawk had young ones there on the cliff. When a little boy, my father climbed after them. The big hawk ran after him. The young hawk spoke to him: "You see my home here. You see what is running out of it. You see blood running down over it and over me. You will be the same way. You may bleed, you may be bloody, but you will not be hurt. You will not die."

This was my father's power. He told it to his people and felt better. He rode off with them. After awhile he got sick of it and died [became unconscious]. He came to again and said: "I have another power."

The one power was not strong enough. A little below Celilo [Falls?] there is a rock called: *Ououts*. There somebody had laid a little salmon under the side of the rock and it had dried to bone and skin. Little Indian boys played with bows, and arrows made from rye grass. They had shot the rye grass arrows into this dried salmon and left them there.

This thing (salmon) said to my father: "Look at my body. It is full of arrows, but they do not hurt me. You will be like me. I will give you my power, and although the arrows strike you, and stay in you as thick as they are in me, they will not hurt you. Nothing will kill you. Do as I tell you and the arrows cannot do you harm. I am not sick from these arrows."

My father did as the dried salmon told him, followed the rules which it gave him; and the arrows were in him just as his power told him, but they did not kill him.

They brought him to Warm Springs [Reservation?], pretty badly off. The arrows were still in him, stone-headed. He suffered a great deal. If I was playing from the tepee, and father would get sick, he would say: "Where is my son?" If father was nearly dead, I would have to lay on his breast. Then he would recover and come to.[168] I know not how I came by my power. He may have given me his power, for I saved him by lying on his breast. I am almost blind, and I see but little; but if war was to come, I would have to go. I would not stand back.

[McWhorter appends here his questions and their answers as given by Histo;]

McWhorter: "I will go with you. Your power must be great, for you went through the wars and did not get hurt."

Histo: "I am glad to hear you say that. Tell me

your power, and I will tell you mine."

McWhorter: I told him the story of one of my ancestors, who was captured by the Indians and lived with them so long that he became thoroughly Indianized; that he could go through the woods when the leaves were dry, without making any noise; that he was a great hunter and a brave man; that I had inherited his Indian power.

Histo: Histo listened attentively and said: "That is a good story. Your power is good, and mine is the same as yours. My father told me his power before he died, and he gave me his power. It is strong. I wear the wings of the "rock hawk" tied to my hair on back of my head when in war, and nothing can hurt me."[169]

McWhorter: Why were the arrows broken off instead of being pulled out of the wounds?

Histo: They were both strong men and did it to see how much they could stand. Nine arrows and three bullets were in my father. The bullets were from another fight. All were in him and [were] buried with him. After he had been dead for some time, his body was gotten out and looked over. When the skeleton was taken up, the arrows and bullets were found still there.

He died of consumption, after middle age. He was in fights after being shot with the nine arrows.

The other man died afterwards. He was this way. A wild horse was tied to a tree. This man came along, and someone called out: "Look out! He will kick you. If you go up to him, you will get kicked."

The man went up to him [the horse], and caught him; and the horse kicked no more. It was his power.

When he thought of his power and did not do right, he had to be hit from behind with a rock until blood ran out of his mouth, before he would quit sinking [?]. He died years afterwards from sickness. He was not killed.

[Explanation by the Interpreter: Wasco Jim]:

Wasco Jim: If an Indian tells of his power and does not do right, he falls flat on the ground. It was this way with the man spoken of. His name was *Klish-tow-wis* which is only a name and no particular meaning.

Power can be derived from any object. I have this fountain pen. You do not see what it contains. I write words with it. The words seem to come from the pen and not me. This is the same as power contained in any object. You cannot see the power, but it is there as in this pen. They speak to us as this pen seems to speak to you. You understand the pen. It is the same with Indians. They can understand what is spoken by other objects. This is the best way that I can explain to you how we understand these things. They are true, and we can understand them well.

33. YAKIMA *TAHMAHNAWIS* POWER; *KAMIAKEN'S* SON[170]

Kamiaken's son, when a small lad, was sent into the mountains in search of a *tah*, or secret power, or *tahmahnawis*. He found and occupied an old Indian hunter's camp, long since abandoned. In previous years a hunter had killed a deer and roasted some of the meat, leaving the bones scattered about the camp. During the night a terrific electric storm camp up, fraught with a great wind, pouring rain, and beating hail.

As the boy crouched under the frail shelter of brush and bark, he heard a voice from out the tempest speaking to him: "You do as I tell you, and I will give you my power. You see that I am old and all weather-checked, but this hail does not enter me nor hurt me. I resist the beating hail stones which beat upon me without harm. Do as I tell you, and with my power, although the bullets of the enemy strike you like a hail storm, you will not be harmed."

The voice then gave certain instructions and rules to be followed, along with a song to be sung in time of danger. These rules and the song were not to be made an idle jest by repeating them unreservedly. Only during ceremony and times of danger, were they to be invoked.

The young Indian followed strictly the injunction, and when he grew to manhood and became a warrior, his body was immune to the arrows and bullets of the enemy. At one time during the War of 1855, this young man with several others were corralled by troops in a deep canyon. It was necessary for a runner to sally forth and bring help. This could not be accomplished without exposure to the [rifle] fire of the soldiers.

It was then that young *Kamiaken* stood forth, proclaiming his ability and intention of leaving the death-trap, and on the run to the camp. He called on his *tah*, sang its song, then dashed out on his horse, receiving without injury the concentrated fire of the enemy. His clothing was riddled by bullets, not one of which penetrated his body.

The *tah*, or *tahmahnawis* which young *Kamiaken* received at the deserted camp, was conferred by one of the dried and weathered deer bones, which had spoken to him during the blackness of the storm. When morning came, he found the bone at the spot where the voice had been heard, and at once knew that it was his good *tahmahnawis*.

I [L.V. McWhorter] have known one Indian, an aged Wishram whose *tahmahnawis* power was contained in a slender braid of his own hair—or even a single hair hanging down in front of his face during battle. So long as this braid, or single hair remained untouched by bullet or arrow, that long was the warrior safe and free from injury by the enemy. But woe to him [when] that hair became severed by an enemy missile. This power was given the warrior when a child hunting his *tah*. It was conferred by a very large woman who appeared to him in a vision.

TAHS WHICH LOCATE GAME

34. *TAHMAHNAWIS* POWER[171]

Spec-hi-low-i-skes-het ("Five Shades," or "Five Shadows") a Umatilla medicine man still living, was hunting with other Indians when it was debated as to the probable location of game. Five Shades declared that if the hunters would assist him, he could tell whether there was any game within the radius of the territory in question.

The men agreed and, procuring sticks and a "sounding" timber on which to beat, they proceeded to sing and beat on the "sounder" in the usual way as practiced when the sick are being treated.

Five Shades with closed eyes began singing his *tahmahnawis*, invoking the aid of its power. Within a few moments he called to some of the men to hold his head, preventing him from moving from his place where kneeling, as he proceeded to feel and grope with his hands for the game.

After groping in every direction, he announced results of his [envisioning] in this wise: "A bear and her two children are off in the hollow place beyond that ridge yonder. You can go kill them, and then quit. There are no deer anywhere around here. The three bears are all that you will find in this part of the country."

The hunters did not believe him, but finally agreed to go to the place where the bears were supposed to be feeding. If found as predicted, then they would believe Five Shades and repair to another locality for hunting.

They went and, sure enough, found the old bear and the two cubs as described by Five Shades. The animals were dispatched; and the party [hunters], being convinced of the fallacy of further hunting in those woods, decamped to other quarters.

35. THE OWL AS A GUIDE OF THE HUNTER IN QUEST OF DEER[172]

The late Chief *Sluskin* understood the language of the owl. The owl would ofttimes inform him in what part of the woods, what section of the mountain vastness the deer would be found on the following day. The hunter never failed of a successful kill when he followed the directions of his night friend. Why was this?

The owl is fond of meat. If a deer was killed, he would always find some portion of it left for him. The chief always remembered his feathered benefactor with the kidneys of his kill. This was all that the owl desired, all that he wanted for his services.

36. A STRANGE INCIDENT
IN *TAHMAHNAWIS* POWER[173]

An Indian of the Yakimas was camping with his wife and her grandmother in the region of Mount Adams during berry season, himself devoting much of his time to hunting. One evening his wife suddenly sniffed the air and remarked to the grandmother: "William has killed a bear. I smell it, and I am going to be sick."

She immediately lay down and was seriously ill for some five days.

Strange as it may appear, her husband had shot and killed a black bear the very instant that she felt the illness coming to her, and at the instant that she declared that she could smell the bear. The husband was fifteen miles from camp when he killed the bear. This is only a part of the strange story. The mother of the wife was at home eighty miles distant, and she knew that something was seriously wrong with her daughter. So positive was she of this fact that she rode all the way to the mountain camp to see her daughter and care for her.

The daughter has the power of the black bear, hence the trouble. She dares not make any use of the flesh of the bear as food. I [L.V. McWhorter] know these people well.[174]

PREMONITIONAL *TAHS* & OMENIC DREAMS

37. SECOND SIGHT OF *WAL-A- MUSK'-KEE*[175]

A. *Wal-a-musk'-kee* is a professional among the Yakimas whose business is to disinter and rehabilitate with new clothing and blankets, the bodies of the dead; to locate lost graves, and to remove bodies from one cemetery to another; ofttimes "bundle" burying the bones of entire families, and groups of relations or kinfolks.[176]

His faculty for finding graves given up as hopelessly lost is a known fact with tribesmen, his mode of procedure bordering on the improbable.

In telling me [L.V. McWhorter], he said: When I am called to exhume a dead body for the purpose of reinterring it in new blankets, and perhaps a new box or casket, I repair the evening before to the house of those wanting my help, and stay with them overnight. I keep my mind strongly on what I am to do the next day. I eat no supper; I go to bed and sleep.

During my sleep—I am not awake—I find myself in the graveyard where I am to work. I see the spirit-people; the very people that I am to take from the graves. I see everything as it really is; the graves singly and in clusters. I see the people plainly and

well. They are happy and glad that I am to help them
to new clothes. Often, they talk to me; telling me how
pleased they are that I have come to help them, to
make them again warm with new blankets.

Others again I see poorly clad; perhaps naked
and shivering with cold. They look pitiful and sad,
because there is no one to help them; no one to redress
their bodies. When you give or replace old blankets
with new, the spirit receives the blanket, although the
blanket remains with the body in the grave. That is the
only way that I can express it. The spirit gets the use
of the blanket, but not the very blanket itself. So with
any object given the dead, of whatever nature.

B. Once an old man had been buried, wrapped in
blankets and matting only. I was sent for to take the
body up and place it in a box with new blankets. The
interment had then been two years. I saw in my dream
that aged man standing by his grave, wet and muddy,
cold.

He said to me: "I am glad that you are going
to help me. I am so cold all the time. It is well that you
are going to do this for me."

Next morning we went to the *memaloose
illahee*[177]. I had never been there. None but one man
knew where the body had been buried. The people
said that they would send for this man to come and
designate the grave. But I knew the grave soon as I
came near the place.

As I approached, I saw at a distance the old
man standing by the side of his grave. He was just as
I saw him in my dream the night before. He appeared
as distinctly as you see those two men out there in the
field. I knew him.

We went into the burial ground, as [while] one man rode off to bring the one who had helped bury the body. I said that I would not wait, that I knew where to dig.

And I did dig and soon had the remains uncovered. They were wrapped in blankets and matting just as described, and just as I had seen in vision.

When the party [the man] came to point out the grave, he was surprised that I had located it myself. He said: "How is this! How did you do this thing alone?"

I replied: "I know my business! Otherwise I would not be here."

C. Once when at the Warm Springs Reservation, I was asked to help remove some bodies to a new cemetery. I agreed, and so went with the people to stay all night. The next day we worked and unearthed all but the body of one little girl. Her grave was apart from the others, lost. It had never been in the burial ground before (sic), and no one knew nothing [anything] about any part of it. One old man and his wife, people who had done lots of such work were there, but they did not help. We dug in several places, but none were right. The aunt said that a pair of shoes had been placed in the casket with the body, but none could be found. Finally, they asked the old man if he could not help, if he could not point out the right grave.

He got mad, for he had not been employed. He said: "Anybody coming into a *memaloose illahee*, should know his business. He should not be like a fool. I am not correcting anyone. I am not doing the work."

In the evening we quit. The leader said: "All will go home and see what you can find out, what you

can learn. Hold your minds strong on this work.
Determine if we cannot locate the grave. It is here. We
must find it."

I was to leave the reservation the next morning,
but agreed to stay and do what I could. I went home
with one of the men, and took bed early. Soon I fell
asleep, holding my mind on what I was doing; held it
on my work. Then I saw: I was in the *memaloose
illahee*, spirit people all around there. They were
happy! Happy because we had brought them new
blankets and clothes. I saw in the graves, saw plainly
and no mistake. And out to one side, out where there
was sagebrush, and where some old caskets were
piled, I saw the little girl.

She said to me: "I am so lonely out here! I
cannot see anything for the brush, for the old boxes
piled on my grave. I want to be over there with those
other people. I am glad that you have come to help
me."

Next morning we went back to the burial
ground. The head man began asking each one what he
knew, what he had seen in his dreams. None knew
anything, had seen nothing. Only one man said that he
had been on the right trail, but was thrown off. Then
I was asked if I had seen anything.

I replied: "Yes! I have seen what I now know.
I saw everything here: the graves, the people buried.
There! That grave you think to be that of the child we
want, is not the one. I see the red and blue beads in that
grave. That other grave you want to open, I see red
blankets there. But out yonder, out there in the sage
where those old caskets are piled, there is the grave
that you want!"

They looked at me. Then one of them said: "No! Here is the grave we want."

They opened the grave that I first mentioned. There were the red and blue beads. They opened the second grave. The red blanket was there. Then they went off to another part of the grounds to dig. I walked over to the pile of empty caskets, removed them, and saw the top of a casket exposed. It was a very shallow burial. I soon had it uncovered and opened. There were the shoes spoken of by the aunt. I called the people who came and saw that I had dreamed correctly. Soon as I had gone to the place and began handling the broken caskets, the old man and his wife took their horses and rode away.

D. An aged man had been buried at White Swan fourteen years. His people desired his body reinterred in a different part of the cemetery. None knew where the grave was located, but his son remembered that a brass plate had been placed on his coffin. I was sent for. I went to the son's house as customary. I did not eat supper. I fixed my mind firm and strong on the work before me. I lay in bed awake for a long time, then I slept. I saw in a dream, in a vision the graveyard and all of its buried dead. Out at one side, apart from the others, I saw an old man sitting lonely by his grave. His face was turned sidewise from me, but I knew at once that there was the grave sought, the body to be removed.

The next morning the son said to me: "What have you seen? What have you found out?"

I answered: "I have it all now. I know the grave where your father is buried."

We went to the cemetery, and I walked directly

to the grave I had seen in the dream.

The son said: "No! That is not the place. My father was not buried there."

I told him that I was right, and that I would prove it to him. I dug down and found the casket almost gone, but the brass plate was there as I had seen it. The son was then convinced. He knew that the body was that of his father, buried in the lost grave for fourteen years.

MALEVOLENT *TAHS* OF THE YAKIMA SORCERER

38. *TAHMAHNAWIS* POWER[178]

The conversation drifted to the late Chief *Sluskin We-owikt*. Sitting Rock suddenly inquired: "You know what kill *Sluskin*? Why he die?"

"No!" I answered. "I was there often. The Chief had a throat trouble."

For a moment the medicine-man regarded me intently, and then spoke: "I know what kill *Sluskin*! I will tell you what kill him. Not long before *Sluskin* get sick, before he die, this thing happen to me; happen here at my home."

"About daylight one morning I see on fence over there where you see tree, a small person; like Mount Hood people.[179] I see this small person about this high [eighteen inches] come slowly, slowly come on top of the fence. I see his face! I see his clothes. All light color; face light color. I watch that small person come slowly on fence; come to the big gate post [distance one hundred yards]. There he drop down slowly into ground. I see all that.

"I said to my wife: 'Maybe doctor-man come soon! Maybe he try catch me like that!'"

Soon *Skumit* [noted medicine-man] come see me. Come same day I see little person on fence. *Skumit* bring one pipe. I show you that pipe.

Going into the house, the medicine-man [Sitting Rock] brought out a modern, Indian-made stone pipe, of fine texture and light gray in color. Handing it to me, he continued.

When *Skumit* come, he say: "Hello!"

I tell him: "Hello!"

Skumit then say: "Well, my cousin! You Shaker yet?"

I answer Skumit: "Yes. I am Shaker. I believe *Schoc-e-les tom* [deity] all I can."

Skumit then begin smoke this pipe [Sitting Rock imitating]. After he smoke he say: "All you Shakers do not smoke. You scared to smoke?"

I tell *Skumit*: "Yes (sic)! Not me! I not scared to smoke. I smoke sometimes."

Skumit then say to me: "They call you "doctor"! Everybody call you "doctor"! I hear you doctor [sic]."

I then say: "Yes! I cannot help it! I not care how they call me."

Skumit then say: "What you know this morning? What you see this morning? Tell me story."

I tell *Skumit*: "I see this morning something come on fence to my gate. I see it drop down in ground. I think that you!"

Skumit laugh! He laugh loud! Loud! Loud!

I tell him: "You take care yourself! You might be sick bye and bye." I talk that way to *Skumit*. *Skumit* die after that.

When hop-time close, I hear *Sluskin* is sick. When I hear that I say: "Sure! *Sluskin* going die!" I knew what is trouble.

When *Skumit* die, *Sluskin* come see him; see body. *Sluskin* see his spirit; see *Skumit's tah*-spirit. It is nice! Looks fine. *Sluskin* takes that spirit off from *Skumit* [clasps his hand along my throat and breast]; takes it home with him.

In wintertime *Sluskin* die. *Sluskin* had the spirit; had *Skumit's tah*-spirit. That is way *Sluskin* get sick. That is why he die.

Sluskin's son *Nu-ah* doctor his father. He say to *Sluskin*: "You steal somebody's spirit. He kill you sure! You not turn him loose."

That is why he die, *Sluskin*. He could not let that spirit go. If I see *Skumit's* spirit, if I take him, he stay with me forever. He stay with me till I die. It was *Skumit's* spirit, his *tah* I see go in ground. *Skumit* send that spirit to find out if I see it; if I am doctor-man. If you doctor-man, you see him all right. If you not doctor, you cannot see him. I was not scared. If I have children, then it make me scared. If I have children, *Skumit* make them sick. But only myself and woman; nothing scare [I am not scared.]

"What became of that spirit when Chief *Sluskin* died?"

"*Sluskin* die, [so] spirit go back where *Skumit* [originally?] get it," replied the "medicine man" promptly. "But *Skumit*, if he alive, never get it again. Maybe little child get it."

"I get one in Wasco County, Oregon; in mountains where is white clay. If someone take that spirit from me, if you take it from me, I never get it back again. If you are strong, I will die. If I am strongest, you will die. If I die with my spirit, it go back where I get it. If I have son, that spirit knows. It comes to him talking. It may stay with him. *Sluskin* was not strong enough. He die. *Skumit* was [had been] strongest."

I will tell you: my father was doctor; my mother was doctor. My wife's father was doctor; her mother was doctor. Four people! All doctors, strong! They have dinner; all eating. They talk about spirits, about *tah* power. The men get hot. They talk strong. They wrestle with *tah*. One doctor man wrestle his *tah* against *tah* of other doctor. In a half snow, all four doctors die. The women wrestle, but not so hot as men. All close[ly] matched; all killed. If not close matched, only weakest be killed. All time it is that way.

Sometimes *tah* gets best of you, is a bad spirit. It makes you do bad things. You cannot help yourself. If *tah* of doctor-man is bad; then that doctor kills people. His spirit kills people. Maybe doctor-man do not want to kill. Maybe he is good man, only spirit bad. That spirit has best of him.

Two weeks ago one boy come from near Wapato [town]. He tell me: "My grandmother bad sick."

That boy give me one sorrel horse worth fifty dollars. I go with him to Wapato, to where woman is sick. I get there in evening. I look at her. I sit down. Sun is down three hours when I say: "No! She going to die! I got nothing to do. She die soon, or in morning."

That woman was doctor. She had *tah*; strong! Big! She was rich. Two children were sick. That woman help doctor them. Yes! I know what is trouble. Doctor-man steal her spirit. She got to die. She died next morning when sun is half way noon. Big tall woman, strong!

I stay there. I take care of body, keep body three days. Then they bury. I clean out house, kill everything inside that house. Kill everything outside, around that house. I take ten wild rose brush [branches?]. I make two sweep-brooms, one [for] inside, one [for] outside. I sweep all over inside house; drive out all bad spirits. Must drive out all spirits belonging to dead woman.

Then I go outside in nighttime. I see all! I see where dead woman has been. Tracks shine light. I hit tracks with rose-brush broom. I kill the tracks. Where dead woman spit, it shines. I see it, kill it with rosebrush. Everything like that I kill, drive away. Make to forget all about dead woman. She is gone.

For all this hard work for doctor, they let me keep the fifty dollars. If I do not [do] this work, then I must give back the money. I did not save the woman; did not hold her life in her body. This is old Injun law. Not like white doctor. He make you pay if you die, same as if you live. Not right to do this. Now, some Injun doctors learn this trick from white doctor. They keep some pay. But old Injun law says not pay if man or woman die.

After I kill all spirits of dead woman, I come back to White Swan. There I see big injun doctor, big man. He say to me: "I hear you doctor one woman?"

I answer him: "Yes!"

Then he ask me: "What kill her?"

I tell him: "That woman not sick. Spirit taken

from her. That is why she die."

That doctor then said: "Yes! That was me! I do that myself."

I ask him:" Why did you do that?"

He answer me: "She high-toned! Saucy! She too smart. I make her stop."

He laughed! That big doctor laughed. He had been where the two children [had been] sick; children doctored by the woman. That doctor-man helped doctor the same children.

39. THE MEDICINE MAN'S MODE OF OBTAINING HEALING POWER[180]

The path of the medicine man is not an easy one, nor is it a trail easily achieved. His "power" must be obtained at great cost and sacrifice. Ofttimes a "power" becomes mischievous and dangerous, beyond the control of its possessor. If in the outset a medicine man loses a patient or two, his *tahmahnawis* is bad, and he has no hold upon it by which he might keep it in subjection, where it could be used to the betterment of his fellowman. Instead, the *tah* or "power" takes the ascendancy and is beyond the keeping of the medicine man and is a thing of dread and evil. It will cause its possessor to kill his own offspring, nor has he any voice in the businesss. He is as helpless as a criminal in the toils [tolls] of the law. I [McWhorter] am acquainted with a good old man, a reputed medicine man who is cursed with an evil "power." Two of his own children and numerous relatives and friends have been sacrificed by this baleful *tah*. Nor can the old man help himself. His own son, when stricken, and knowing what was being done, sprang for his rifle and would have killed his father had not his wife interfered and seized the gun.

When a man aspires to become successful in the career of healing by occult power, he, or she arranges a great potlatch and feast and all friends are invited. A close friend of mine [not identified], who has been more or less successful in the profession of a medicine man, when entering on his career as such, made a five days' and five nights' festival, where a wagon-load of blankets and calicoes were distributed, and where the provisions cost him $150.00. In addition to the dry goods given away, the gifts included many articles of Indian manufacture and five head of horses.

In this case it is interesting to note that the number of days and nights, and the number of horses correspond to the "five laws" or "rules of Coyote."[181] The more expended in gifts which really is in the nature of an invocation to *Me-yay'-yah*, the greater will be the medicine man's control over his *tahmahnawis* power. While this five days' preparation cost the aspirant several hundreds of dollars, it all came back to him from his devotees. His fees consist of cattle, horses, cash, Indian manufactured goods, and blankets. He is regarded as an honest man, and I believe that he is sincere in his belief and work.

When the wife of Chief *We-yal-lup Wa-ya-cika*, was fatally ill, several of the most noted of the Yakima medicine men were present, and among them this particular man. The other men, through jealousy or other cause, opposed him, and through secret machinations their "powers" were about to overcome,

smother the "power" of the envied one, when he
caused his "power" to ascend into the air far overhead
where it could not be discovered by the enemy
"powers." This incident was told me [L.V. McWhorter]
by the medicine man in question; and he told me of a
distant medicine man who knew of the terrible straits
to which he had been placed, although seventy miles
away. Not withstanding this distance, the friendly
medicine man sent his own power to the rescue of his
friend.

40. DEATH OF _PI-A-KOTES_[182]

Pi-a-kotes was a medicine man of good repute,
residing on the Colville Reservation. He was often
called to great patients among the Yakimas, with some
of whom I am well acquainted. He possessed two
tahmahnawis "powers": one was that of the great
horned _wah'k-puch_ chief; the other a white horse.
Coffee, a rival medicine man, also possessed two
"powers": that of the bullsnake, and that of a great
buffalo bull.

One day, as _Pi-a-kotes_ was returning home
from a two days' treatment of a patient, he was riding
ahead of his wife who had accompanied him. His
route passed the home of _Coffee_ who watched him
from concealment in his corral shed. As _Pi-a-kotes_
was passing a tree which grew by the roadside, the
bullsnake _tahmahnawis_ [of _Coffee_] leaped upon him
from the trunk of the tree. _Pi-a-kotes_ felt the power
strike him, felt that he had been struck by something
bad. But he continued on home where he immediately

went to bed.

He grew worse day after day, although different medicine men were called in to treat him. The white horse *tahmahnawis* [belonging to *Pi-a-kotes*] had escaped when the first attack occurred. This alone had prevented a speedy death.

Pi-a-kotes gradually sank under the baleful power of the bullsnake *tahmahnawis*, but [his own] white horse power kept him alive.

Finally, *Coffee* sent his buffalo bull *tahmahnawis* to the attack. This spirit-power saw the white horse power standing outside, in the open; charged it, and killed it. This was the finish of *Pi-a-kotes*, who immediately died.

41. *TAHMAHNAWIS* POWER OF *LAUX-WOPTUS*[183]

It was berry time in the mountains. An aged medicine man of the Yakimas and wife, in preparing for the annual outing, were short of both supplies and ready money. In their extremity they applied to *Laux-woptus* who had a small store, but were refused credit. After an argument the old man grew angry and exclaimed: "Keep your supplies! But they will do you no good. You will never get any benefit from them."

Laux-woptus made solemn reply: "I am a stronger medicine man than you. Go on to the mountains! Make the trip! But you will not be permitted to taste one berry. You will be carried out of the mountains."

Scared, the woman remonstrated at so dire a

sentence.

Laux-woptus retorted: "You heard my words! Go! You will have to get help to carry your man back home for burial."

The old couple made the journey to the berry field, but, strange to say, the [old] medicine man immediately fell ill and died before tasting any of the coveted fruit. This occurrence firmly established the reputation of *Laux-woptus* as a powerful medicine man; not only among the Yakimas, but with all the kindred tribes as well.

42. MEDICINE MEN OF THE YAKIMAS[184]

There are, at this time at least fourteen or sixteen "medicine" men and women on the Yakima Indian reservation. Sam *Poyat*, residing in the Medicine Valley, has for some years posed as the foremost among them as the most potentially strong, but of late his prestige is waning. This is attributed to a diminution of occult "power," rather than otherwise. Age, however, is a recognized factor in the decline of curative, or healing powers.

The first of the present month—April—a prominent tribeswoman grew suddenly and critically ill near White Swan, a reservation village. A white M.D. was summoned who pronounced her malady to be fatal. *Poyat* was summoned. He was offered six good-sized cows; three good teams of two horses each, heavy work horses; several shawls, blankets, and some beaded goods if he would save the woman. For four days he labored over her, backed by a goodly number of "stick-pounders"[185] and the accustomed "repeater" or "helpers,"[186] but to no purpose. The woman died. Four other women died about the same time, attributable to a malicious *tahmahnawis*, possessed by an evil medicine man. These women had engaged in a gambling game during an entire night at the Long House, and were chilled. They had drank from a recently emptied tin can which had contained prepared vegetables, and doubtless were killed by ptomaine poisoning, as attributed by the more intelligent Indians.

43. SEEDS OF DEATH WITHIN THE BODY DISCERNED BY THE MEDICINE MAN [TO BE] SHINING OR BLAZING LIKE FIRE[187]

A man may be stricken unconsciously with the seeds of death. He may pass by a medicine man though wrapped in his blanket. The gifted one can see this death flame as if in the open. In the head, breast, stomach, or other parts of the body, it is plainly within the sight of the medicine man. He may shake hands with the doomed one, tell him that he is not looking well, but he dares not inform him of what is in immediate store for him. If he does, it will rebound to his own hurt.

This *tah*, or *tahmahnawis* is a very dangerous element, which may get the upperhand of the one possessing it, making him subservient to a bad purpose even against his will. His *tah* may become a "killing" *tah*, in which case the man cannot help killing people. Such medicine men have no curative powers. They are only to kill.

44. A *TAHMAHNAWIS* INCIDENT[188]

Chief *We-yal-lup Wa-ya-cika* was gambling with bones against two medicine men of an Oregon tribe. It was test of the power of the *tahmahnawis* of the three wizards.

The Yakima Chief, *We-yal-lup*, called upon his rattlesnake *tah* so successfully, that his two rivals were made to see rattlers within the space separating the players. The serpents would appear first with heads slightly raised above ground, but as the game waxed hotter and hotter, they became more pronounced, rearing their forms two feet in the air.

These phantom rattlers were visible only to the medicine men, the other players remaining in ignorance of their presence. The Yakima carried off the spoils.

MISCELLANEOUS *TAHS*

45. *TAHMAHNAWIS* POWER[189]

A band of Umatilla hunters were in camp. A great eagle circled and soared overhead, far up in the skies. An aged *tahmahnawis* man was challenged to bring down the eagle with his *Tah*.

He said: "I can do that." The old hunter "shot" his *tahmahnawis* at the bird, but to no purpose. The eagle continued soaring.

It was then that a younger man said: "You are too old.   You cannot kill the eagle with your *tahmahnawis* power. I will now kill the eagle with my power."

Suiting action to his words, the young man "shot" his *tahmahnawis* at the eagle, which immediately came tumbling down through the air, falling dead near the camp. The aged Indian made no comment. He had been beaten by his younger companion.

46. CHIEF *YAL-LUP* AS A MEDICINE MAN, GIVES AN INSTANCE FROM LIFE[190]

The chief said: "My leg was broke[n]. I could get about only slightly. My cousin came and told me: 'A man is dying.'

I went to see him. He was nearly dead. Only a short time to live.

I told my cousin: "I will repeat my *power* and try to cure. If I do not receive a cure [from Yal-lup's *power*], this man will die."

Then I call my *power*—repeat it—for the man is about to die. He got well. He is still living. I saved him. [Told to me in person. L.V. McW.).

PART THREE

CHAPTER SIX

SOME MID-COLUMBIA TRIBAL TALES RECOUNTING THE DEATH JOURNEY VISION[191]

A physician may be no stranger to death, but during 1878 Dr. George B. Kuykendall was witness to a curious envisioning of the afterlife during the dying of a young Indian girl.[192]

In 1878 I witnessed a very interesting ceremony on the occasion of the death of a Wisham [Wishram] chief's daughter. She was a girl of perhaps 18 years [of age] and was dying of typhoid fever. She wanted her friends to gather round and sing the death song and dance. The dancing could scarcely be called a dance, as it was simply a slight bend of the knees and then straightening again, or throwing the weight of the body on the ball of the foot and raising the heel at the same time moving the hands up and down in time to the singing. The dying girl feebly attempted to sing with those who were singing around her in the lodge. Her bed was on the ground floor which was cleanly swept.

She was thus singing and talking at intervals, and feebly moving her hands in time to the tune when I entered the lodge. I went up to her bedside, stooped down, and took one of her hands in mine to examine her pulse. She seemed to want to keep on moving her hand in time with the music. I perceived she was failing [the word *and* has been erased here]: the circulation was growing feeble, and the machinery of life was about to come to a final standstill. Some one [sic] kept ringing a very small bell about twenty inches above her head. When I took hold of her hand, she looked toward me and said something I did not understand. The friends told me she was desirous that I should move my hands in time with the singing. I hesitated, not wishing in any way to lend sanction to their superstitions.

She seemed to be worried that I did not comply with her wishes, and several times repeated her request that I should keep time. She seemed so impatient and anixous [sic] that finally out of pity I complied, and she then expressed great satisfaction at my so doing.

She then talked, and her friends interpreted to me. She said that before the sun went down behind the mountains she would be in the spirit land. She saw [N.B.], standing before her and up above, her mother and other deceased friends. There before her was a beautiful light. She saw the Great Spirit father and the happy people in heaven. Heard bells ringing a welcome to her. Her friends were beckoning her; they all were very happy and the place very beautiful.

She continued to talk and keep time to the music of the wierd [sic] plaintive melancholy death song until her strength failed and she died. They then ceased their sing [sic], and began their lamentations, and to adjust her body for its position in the long death sleep. Thus passed away the spirit of the young and untutored and yet gentle daughter of *Selachie* the Wisham chieftain.

_____

Gathered together here are eleven narratives of *death journey visions*, similar to that of the dying Indian girl, seldom if ever reported from among the American Indian—found, even frequently, among white, European-Americans.[193] Nine narratives of the death journey vision were collected by L.V. McWhorter during the early 20th century, and have not previously been published, that we know.[194]   Likewise, two traditional accounts of the death journey vision were recorded by Leslie Spier.[195]   These death journey visions are provocative, beg critical examination: extensive cultural changes are evident because the persona and power of the shaman are taken on by the visionee; and, not previously evident, a new concept of the after-life for the Indian *and* solace is evident. The vision, however new and culturally unique, is *translated* back into a traditional oral format: the new within the old, reflecting the tenacity of oral tradition.

To properly understand the visions, a brief historical and cultural survey of the Yakimas and the Wishram Indians is necessary. The Yakimas ranged over Central Washington, and the Wishrams dwelt along the north side of the Columbia River eastward from modern The Dalles, Oregon. They were hunter-fishers, in larger or lesser degree depending on the nearness of fish-laden streams to their tribal lands. Only relatively recently having acquired the horse, not especially war-like, except for defensive postures against the Paiute and Bannock tribes of Eastern Oregon and Idaho, these Indians lived quietly. But in

1855 the Yakimas and the Wishrams had a treaty
forced upon them whereby they gave up their vast
lands, and with other tribal entities were moved onto
the confines of the Confederated Tribes and Bands of
the Yakima Indian Reservation. No longer allowed to
fish for salmon or to roam the mountains hunting
game, their languages and heritages dismissed, the
Indians were forced to become farmers, or herdsmen,
do other tasks which their new "homes" would permit.

The white man's religion came early to the
Indians. The "black robes" or Roman Catholic priests
arrived among the Yakimas by 1847. In 1871 following
numerous corrupt reservation Agents, the Rev. J.H.
Wilbur, "Father Wilbur," a Methodist cleric, was
named as Indian Agent and Methodist minister to the
tribe by President U.S. Grant. For nearly two decades
Wilbur ruled the Indians, converting them to Christian
belief, "civilizing" them, honestly conducting the office
of Indian Agent.[196],[197] But the power of the Indians'
traditional religious beliefs remains unmeasured. The
shaman remained a very important figure,[198] and was
rather numerous. According to information obtained
by L.V. McWhorter in 1927, 14 or 16 shamans were
extant on the Yakima Indian reservation.[199] Several
Indian accounts survive describing their belief in an
afterlife. Indeed, to the Yakima immortality and the
afterworld were reached only after extensive travel on
foot or on horseback. To this end, a man's best horse
might be killed at his grave so that a good mount would
be available during the next life. And if the Indian was
evil in life, in death he quickly became lost, wandered
until taken with a spirit of repentance. At that time he
found his way to the spirit world. The spirit land was

not far from the favorite areas of this life where an Indian hunted or loved to be. If the afterworld was idyllic, it resembled what was familiar from life: good water, familiar scenery, game animals and food easily at hand. The following version of immortality was recorded by McWhorter in September 1920, from *I-keeps-swah* (Sitting Rock), whose death journey vision appears hereafter.

"When a man dies, if he has been bad, if he has killed some one or stolen any thing, he will know it when he starts on the trail to the next life. He goes a distance, travels for a time, and then gets lost. He must stay there for many snows; maybe forty snows. It might be a longer time than forty snows, and he is lonely all the time. He sees moccasined footprints on the trail, all going different directions, to different places. There are no guiding rock-signs; nothing to tell him which way to go. He is lost! All this long time, all these long snows, he wanders around. He is lonely; is feeling badly. He wants to see his people, but he stalls on the way.

"Gradually the heart of this trail-bound spiritman makes a change. He is sorry that he ever gambled, that he ever stole. He is sorry that he ever killed somebody. He wants to go somewhere, but can not find his way. Finally he sees horse tracks. He thinks: "Where are my horses? Where's my best horse?"

"When he thinks that, his horse comes to him; comes flying through the air. He gets on that horse, and his horse takes him to the place he wants to go [to]. That place is the Better Land, where the good are living. The horse returns to its own spirit world. The man never sees that horse again. That is the way I have heard it told."

47. "Klikitat-Yakima Belief About After Death" from *Smah-lah-hop*, 1920

The old belief of my people, Klikitat and Yakima, is that after death the spirit rides about this earth on a former favorite horse; the best horse that the man possessed in this life. The two spirits, man and horse, are never again separated. This is why the good horse was killed at the grave of the dead man. Sometimes the skin was removed and spread on top the stakes set in the *yah'-ya-tosh* of the rockslide. But this was not always done. Ofttimes the horse must be sent after its owner without wounds.

The Spirit Land, or "Happy Hunting Grounds," is not off somewhere. It is located where the Indian loved to be in this life. This country was created for him. The afterlife is in this same good country, but it is changed to a spirit world. Everything there is good, with no trouble. The bad is killed at the grave.

48. "Concerning Life After Death" from a Yakima Hunter, April 1921

When I die, I stay right here in dis mountain. I go no where else! Some people go way off some where; go some other country. But dey do not know dis place. I like dis place! High mountains, big rocks; good water. I stay right here all time.

49. "More About the Spirit World"
from a Yakima chief, 1922

Spirit World much like this life, only everything
good. Nothing bad! Animals there, same as Injuns.
Everything you like to eat. It is there! But you do not
kill as in this life. You wish for Yah'-mas, the deer
comes to you. You take what you want; cut it with
spirit knife. The deer does not feel any hurt. No wound
as hunting here. The spirit-deer remains sound and
whole. Cut of the knife passing, instantly heals. No
blood, no pain. No death comes to the Spirit World.

For Indian youth, including girls, an extensive
physical and emotional preparation toward perceiving
visions culminated in the *tahmahnawis* [*tah*] or spirit
quest. First, while still very young the youth listened
closely—ingested tribal lore, including lore of animal
sources of spirit power, from the elders. Failure to pay
close attention brought harsh punishment.[200],[201]
Second, the youngster listened to others' accounts of
tah power related at the winter dances, or at the
"coming out" of the *tah*-quest-completing-youth. Thus,
the youngster furnished his mind with the images,
details for his own subsequent vision.[202] Third, for the
youth "social expectation" likely played some role,
because the "coming out" of the successful *tah* quester
was marked by celebration and gift-giving.[203] Fourth,
explicit preparation for the youth included ordeals to
prepare him/her for the spirit quest soon to occur. The
youth might be directed to a remote site where sans
food, light or fire, he was to perform a task. Or he

might be directed to seek out a particular cavern by a dark riverside, and to dive into its unknown, murk-shrouded depths.[204]   Lastly, the actual *tah* quest followed. The youth was led to a very distant point, perhaps given a task to accomplish during one or more days and nights. The youth was required to go without food, have no fire or light, and to stay awake. Usually, in a dream an animal or other entity would appear to the youth, teach him or her a magic song, and then depart. But that animal or entity would serve the youth throughout life according to the animal's peculiar spirit power. However, not all Indian youth succeeded at receiving a *tah* spirit.[205],[206]

With condemnation of the old religious beliefs of the Indians by white reservation authorities came the rise of *Smohallah* worship. *Smohallah* worship was a *visionistic* reassurance of ultimate defeat of the whites when the Indians might once more resume their old ways. *Smohallah* worship represented a retreat from the Indians' defeat, their subsequent maltreatment and hardship in transition to reservation life. In 1924 Leslie Spier, p. 251, reported:

"The *Smohallah* cult still flourishes on the Yakima Reservation in the form of the *Pom-pom* or Feather religion. It still has its adherents among the handful of Wishram and Wasco, but many of them, perhaps the majority, are converts to Methodism and that pseudo-Christian sect of the Pacific Northwest, the Shakers." Spier continues, ". . . the historic cults, *Smohal-lah*, *Pom-pom*, Shakers, and the two Ghost Dance movements, were merely so many special expressions of an old form of revelatory religion that prevailed in this general area. [It] . . . indicates a recurring pattern of behavior, the specific instances of which cannot be easily assigned to one or another of the historic cults. "

Accordingly, the visions examined in this volume relate, we believe, less to *Smohallah* than to a larger cultural and traditional context—*and change*.

The eleven death journey vision accounts appearing hereafter share similar anthropomorphic imagery of life after death: the traditional and new, the fearsome and delightful. To all outward appearances only No. 50 ("Dream Presentment of Death") retains traces of traditional Yakima notions of death and the hereafter, an "old vision" according to some traditional accounts.[207] In particular here the dying person does not travel, but a band of Indians, old friends and kin from the land of the dead (*memmaloose Illahee*), comes to her, circles her house three times, and then departs. By contrast, a "new vision" might include No. 58 ("A Border Vision") hereafter in which a Roman Catholic has fallen away from the church, has joined the Indian Shaker Church. But, now, falling gravely ill, she experiences a vision wherein she eats at a "filthy, greasy table; eating cooked (*Wah'k-puch*) rattlesnake."[208] The substance of her frightful vision compels her to renounce her new-found faith and to return to her former Roman Catholic beliefs and practices, that the priest might bless her, "that I may die holy."

Some of the visions are fearsome indeed. For example, in vision No. 52 ("Vision of _____,"); also No. 53 ("Vision of *I-Keeps-Swah* {Sitting Rock})" hereafter, the frightening picture of a Hell or "Sheol" is evident much as promised in *Revelations*, 9.1-2, also 19.20-21. According to these visions, the last days of the earth will be given over to violent earthquakes; the earth will become "hot, hot, hot" [molten?]. But still other accounts reveal a picture of eternity not seen or heard directly, but hinted at as paradisiacal. As in No. 54 ("Vision of Charley _____,") the dying person discovers a "beautiful country," green, with lush grasses, berries, thick forests. As the dying person approaches, he perceives a place where people are dancing (or even are heard singing), and from afar he recognizes many people—even relatives—as people who had died many years before. But the dying person is turned back, must return to earth to atone for his past wickedness. After learning one or more magic songs, sadly the dying person returns to life. There he revives from the "dead" and preaches to his people that they must reform, must give up their wicked ways.

The eleven oral accounts of the death journey vision show essentially similar traits to traditional Plateau Indian narratives, even if their content reflects an extraordinary shift of belief. First, the oral accounts of the death journey vision are placed within a frame. Here begin details of a fatal illness or grievous injuries from an accident. And the frame most often closes with the return to life of the deceased and of attempts made to make amends for an ill-spent life. The frame of the story only emphasizes that these traditional accounts are not fanciful but are narrated as entirely serious, factual, truthful accounts. Second, as a result of illness or injury death comes for the protagonist. (While we might quarrel that the Indians' notion of death was merely a comatose, not a proven state of death, we have no easier time at distinguishing final and complete death in spite of all our scientific advancements.) Third, in the statement of the vision, the deceased is usually aware of walking a path which seems to go straight, upward; of discovering a pleasant place much like the countryside surrounding the tribal locale. Fourth, the shaman has been displaced here— the protagonist himself confronts the Great Spirit. Usually the deceased meets a "person" who is not identified, most often is merely a voice, and who rejects the deceased for wickedness, and directs him or her to return to earth, and life. Fifth, at this point the "dead" revives, regains consciousness. The deceased is usually perceived to regain consciousness by those watching nearby over the remains. Indeed, the Indians' great reluctance to bundle their dead in blanketry for final entombment is noted by Spier.[209] But with revival, and perhaps upon receiving food, the revived person catechizes those about him or her of their sins, of their need to live right. Then, as in No. 60 ("Vision of *Quas-qui Tachens*,") specific persons are named; for having grievously sinned, they will be next to die. All listeners are admonished to abandon errant ways for their own good. Particularly interesting, in several narratives the revived person sings a song which he or she was taught by the "Person on the trail," and we might infer parallel with the *tah* song learned as a youth.[210] Such a song must have played no small part in validating the death journey experience because of where it was learned, by its content. It was sung to the revived person's audience, the several families of young and old, crowded about in the dim atmosphere of the winter longhouse, the wintry winds howling outside.

Although the preaching by the Roman Catholic and Methodist missionaries may have contributed to the death journey vision among the Indians, yet a more encompassing influence remains—oral tradition. Following this chapter traditional motifs are listed for each death vision. For this I have employed Thompson, Stith 1955-58. *Motif-Index of Folk-Literature. . ..* Bloomington: Indiana University Press. And I have also relied upon Thompson, Stith 1966. *Tales of the North American Indian.* Bloomington: Indiana University Press. In this manner, traditional details of character, plot, or background detail are noted which occur in the narratives. While I have not attempted any measurement, a high incidence of *meshing* occurs between motifs found within these narratives, and with motifs previously occurring in oral literatures from over Europe and other regions. Thus we infer that the great body of oral tradition, as exemplified by folkloric motifs, and extending worldwide, played no small part in these texts within oral traditions of the Yakimas, Wishrams, and elsewhere.

The death journey vision narratives of the Mid-Columbia River Indians, as with the envisioning of the dying young girl, employ a traditional narrative form with a new belief content. Traditionality of the texts is attested by the traditional motifs, and the close parallels of the texts with Olrik's Epic Laws.[211] More, within a narrative frame an opening and a closing device occur (a recounting of a personal odyssey at death, but a forced return to the living and confession— even atonement for past wrongs). Indeed, the vision narrative may be a cultural mechanism of solace, of reassurance against the frightening, the unknowable of dying.

According to Dr. G.B. Kuykendall's observations of the milieu about the dying young girl, the death vision journey provides a brief glimpse at extraordinary tribal cultural change underway. Indeed, with the 1855 treaty creating the Confederated Tribes and Bands of the Yakima Indian Nation, and grouping together its dissimilar tribal groups—great cultural stress was induced. Even by Kuykendall's time tribal languages and cultures began to deteriorate; for ca. 25 years the bands and other tribes now comprising the Confederated Tribes and Bands of the Yakima Indian Nation were closely intermingled so that gradually their cultures and linguistic boundaries were becoming indistinct. A number of nations (the Wenatchi, Wishrams, Wanapums and others) were forced onto the Yakima Reservation. Probably the lesser tribes conformed to the stronger Yakima tribe—and the language and the culture loss among the lesser tribes was most likely much greater. The pervasive influence of the English language existed: the language of business, justice, and of claims for/against the government, the schools on the reservation, also the white man's religion by which one's soul was saved from certain hellfire [the Indian's languge and ways were proclaimed by whites as the ways of the devil]. Cultural release from stress took place in varieties of change, especially apostate change as exemplified in the death vision journey narratives. A final example of the extraordinary tribal cultural changes can also be seen especially in Kuykendall's narrative. To be sure, familiar details from tribal life and locale may indeed dress a vision, but the visions detail a new form of the hereafter. Both a paradisiacal as well as a hellish locale are now cited, and the frightening prospect of being rejected, of being forced to return to life is recounted. But absent is the shaman. Instead, the offices of the shaman have been assumed by the dying person herself, as Kuykendall recounts. No magic, or intermediary's employment of familiars; but the power of the "new religion" is most frequently at work. Not the shaman but the dying person either contacts or addresses directly "the great Spirit Father." And not the shaman but the dying is allowed a glimpse of the "spirit land."

The following accounts of dying, and of departure from life on a death journey are arranged in chronological order. Titles for each narrative are those given by McWhorter, Spier or others. The informant, date when the narrative was written down, and other details as McWhorter's or Spier's notes will allow are given. Finally, McWhorter's original language and narrative format have been retained. Where needed, correct spelling, punctuation, and grammar have been inserted for clarity.

50. DREAM PRESENTIMENT OF DEATH

An-a-whoa, or *An-awho-ee* (Black Bear), narrator of "Bridge of the Gods" legend,[212] died during August 1918, after a long and continued illness. Three days prior to her death, she told her daughter and son-in-law the following.[213]

Last night I was sleeping. I dreamed! And this

is what I saw in that dream. I saw my people! My old people! Those when we lived in the long-lodge, an entire band together. They have long since gone to the *memmaloose illahee* (land of the dead), but last night they came back to me. I saw them as in other suns; as in other snows. They passed by the sun-rise [east?] window, where I stood. I watched them pass,[214] circling the house three times, as when the dead are taken away for burial. Some were [on] horseback, some on foot. I gazed on them filing by in silence. They did not look my way, did not notice me. Three times they circled the house. Three times they shadowed the window, then were gone. I did not see their going. They only faded from my sight.

I was glad to see them, my own old people. I know what it means, why they came. I will not be here many more suns. I want to be ready. I must be clean and ready to go. Get water! Let me bathe. I will dress in fresh clothes. I will be ready to go."

Water was provided; and although very ill and suffering from weakness, the aged woman bathed; donned her best clothing, and lay down content. On the third morning from [after] her vision, she was dead.

An-a-whoa was almost blind at the time of her death.

51. VISION OF AN AGED
WARM SPRINGS WOMAN

A woman who had seen many snows died but returned to life again.[215] She described the wonderful things that she had seen. She spoke of how she had recognized her departed children, who came to meet her on the trail. But it was revealed to her that none would be permitted to recognize their children [parents?] unless they had lived correct lives on earth. Among other things that she heard in [was] the Voice of an unseen personage, were these song-words.

"It is a beautiful
thing when our children
    come to meet us,
        But we may not know
our children; may never
           know them."

52. VISION OF _____ [216]

[According to McWhorter: This young man had lost both feet in a railroad accident, caught on the bridge while drinking, at Fall Bridge, {the modern town of Wishram} Washington. Recovering, he thought to show his prowess in riding an outlaw horse, was thrown and "killed" for a time. During his insensibility, he saw this vision]:

A straight trail appeared before me, and I was instructed by the voice of a speaker whom I could not hear [perhaps see?] to walk on this trail. It led out into a fine looking country. On either side there were great clustering berries, bending the bushes with their weight. And there were all kinds of edible roots, some flowering—and everything was fine.

Then the Voice said to me: "See! This has been your first wrong! You have never attended the feasts of your people in the partaking of the First Foods. You did not believe in such things. You did very wrong when you made light of this old, and fine custom of your people."

I went on and soon saw a white woman standing before me on the trail. I knew her! I had slept with that woman.

She smiled at me, said to me: "You cannot pass me!"[217]

Then the Voice spoke to me again: "See! This is your second wrong. You should not have done this thing with that woman. It was a great wrong for you to do so. Pass her, go around her on the trail."

I walked around her and went on. Soon I saw a black woman standing in my way, just as stood the white woman. I recognized her as a woman I had been with.

The Voice spoke: "There was your third great wrong. You should not have done as you did with this woman who was not of your race. She stands in your way to the Good Land. But walk around her and go on!"

I walked around her and left her on the trail. Soon I came where I could see an Indian woman lying exposed with feet towards me, with a great dog, sheared like a lion, walking around her, barking in a fierce and fighting manner. This dog was guarding her and came nearly biting me. He was savage! I knew this woman as the wife of another man—and whom I had been with. Like the white woman, she is still living.

The Voice again spoke to me, "This was another great wrong which you did. You were with this woman who sleeps with a dog. She has the dog as her man. She is in your way forever. Go around her on the trail!"

I went around this woman and her dog and came to where I saw an Indian woman sitting on a stone by the trail. At this place there were many trails, all leading out in various directions. This woman must sit there in the semi-darkness until she learned which way to go; until she became good enough to take the right trail. I saw an Indian whom I know, who is still alive, named *Spear*. He was at one side and I called out to him, "Hello, *Spear*! Which trail must I take to get to the Good Land?"

"Take the left-hand trail, over this way. That is the one to take you to the Good Land."

I followed on this left-hand trail and soon came into a fine, wide country, everything the most beautiful I ever had imagined. I cannot describe it. Flowers, roots and berries, everything good; and it was lit up like lamplight. I looked and soon I saw snakes, the *Wah'k-puch* and frogs coming over the land thick, all squir-ming and twisting in a scary manner. Then up arose beings like humans with bones in their mouths, gnawing them; meat in their mouth, eating it. Those bones and that meat were human remains. The people were eating such.

While I looked, scared and trembling, I heard a great loud noise, yelling and wrangling; the people fighting each other. Then a big voice spoke behind me, "I am King! Come, boys, and play cards with me. If I win, you are mine! If you win, you go free; you do not have to stay here."

I turned and saw a giant man, big and strong, sitting down. He was shuffling cards and continued calling to the people to come and play cards with him.

Then I knew! I had always played cards, and I knew that I was to stay where I then was. While I listened to the wild yells and the screams of the fighters; listened to the challenging of the King for his people to come play with him, I heard a greater noise off somewhere above and in the distance, a noise unlike that about me. It was music of some kind, fine and good to hear. It was made up of happy voices, something not like anything of earth.

While I stood listening to this finest of sounds, the Voice again spoke: "There! You can hear, but you cannot see or go to the place where the good people are. It is their voices that [you] now hear. They are in the better Spirit Land. But you can not go there as you now are. You must return to life; and if you avoid the bad things which you have been shown on the trail, if you do the good things as shown you, then, when you die again, you can go where the happy ones are. But if you do not live right, if you continue in the bad way, then you will forever have to remain with the bad things you have seen here, with those who are not permitted to go to the Happy Land."

"Go back, now, to your earthlife and wait till you are called again."

Then I awoke, came to life again, all trembling and badly scared. I determined never to play cards nor do the things as shown me to be bad. I lived right for a time, but the boys got me to playing cards again, and now I suppose I will have to stop at the wild, fighting place where the giant king was shuffling his cards and calling to the people to come play with him. The only good time for me is while I remain here in this life.

53. VISION OF *I-KEEPS-SWAH*
(Sitting Rock)[218]

[McWhorter notes: In the autumn of 1924, *I-keeps-swah* (Sitting Rock) known as Wasco Jim, and whose Christian name is Jim Peter, was seriously hurt by his runaway team, near the Toppenish Bridge, the Mt. Adams Highway. In telling me of the incident and its subsequent influence over his mind, he said]:

I thought to haul wood and get three hundred, four hundred dollars, whatever I could find, and build a Long House; make a big time and give away everything that I had. This would make me a big doctor [Indian shaman or "power doctor"], and I could make lots of money, get it all back and more, by doctoring the people.

It was September and I was hauling the wood from the hills. Going for a load of logs, I took the bits from my horses' mouths so they could drink at Toppenish Creek. They drank, and I thought to fix the bridles after they had left the water. The horses became scared. They ran away with me in the wagon. When they reached the rocky place up from the creek, the wagon came apart, the reach dropping to the ground. There was nothing on the wagon, for I was only hauling logs and was then going after a load. I was thrown to the ground, a sharp rock striking me here where this scar is in my forehead.

I went to sleep! Then this is what I saw. I saw a white flag [shroud?] being wrapped around me, from my feet all up my body, covering my head and blinding my eyes. I heard somebody say: "Now you go up!" I began going up, up, up! It was a funny feeling!

When I was half way to the sky, I said: "I will stop!" I stopped.

The flag was removed from my eyes, and I heard some one say: "Look down from where you came." I looked down and this earth was hot! Hot! Hot!

I heard again somebody say: "Nine years more and the earth will shake! Shake! Shake! Ten years more and the earth will be as you now see it: hot! Hot! Hot! You will live eight more years and then you will die. Pray to god now! Those who pray to Him when the earth shakes, those who pray to Him when the earth grows hot, He will not hear them. Pray to Him now, for when the earth is hot and the water boils, it will be the last. Now you go back! Do not smoke! Do not booze! Do not doctor! Doctoring is a bad thing, for you take the peoples' money for nothing, stealing it."

Then I came back to earth, not falling hard, but lighting easy and no trouble. I wake up. One man finds me all covered with blood. He said: "You will die!"

I told him: "No! I will not die! I am living eight more years, and then I will die. I have seen the end. I know!"

Now, my friend, I will have seven more years to life when this fall comes. You watch! You count the years. No, I do not care that I am to go! I do not scare because of that time. I am no longer a doctor. I do not smoke. I gave my pipe away. I do not drink whiskey. I am trying to live right. Yes, I am Shaker now. Yes, that is why I cut my hair last September. I am quit [of] all bad things now.

54. VISION OF CHARLEY _____ [219]

[When I died] what I saw, how I felt just before my last breath, was similar to what my people saw [me do?]. I was dead three days. Just before I died, I saw my mother who had died some years before. She was high up in the air. After I died, I saw a beautiful country, with grass knee high and as green as green can be—no brush nor any kind of stick. I walked along until I finally saw some bushes. Reaching these I saw a person standing at the edge of it. I saw these were huckleberry bushes with nice green berries on them. I thought at once that I must pick one and try it.

This person said: "No! You must not pick any of these berries." He was standing right in the pathway. He stepped aside and told me to go on, warning me not to put my fingers on the berries. I heeded and went along.

After a while I came to a place where there were many green fir trees, cedar, and other timber. I saw a person standing there, also in the pathway. Oh, how nice the trees looked. I thought I would take a small limb of one; but before I did, or spoke, this person repeated what the other had said. He gave way to me and I went on, finding at the next place creeks, full of small and large fish; at the following places deer, elk, places with beautiful birds, places with all kinds of roots Indians use as food. At each place was a person in a cave, dressed in deer and elkskin clothing decorated with eagle feathers and painted with yellow paint.

I finally reached a place where people were

dancing, but I was stopped before getting very close. I saw people whom I knew had died years before and my relatives. But no one would speak to me. I tried my best to talk to my dear mother, but she would not even look at me.

I learned the songs they sang and the way they performed. Then I was told by one of the persons that I must do likewise, that I must teach my people this before I would be allowed with them and my mother.

"We will send you back; you are wicked." After talking to me a little, he turned me around to the right.

I woke from death and since then have done as I was told. I will never forget that I have a place to go after my death where I can find my people. I did not see a white person nor any but Indians. Preachers of older days never saw any either. They believed, and I too believe, that white men do not go to the place we Indians go. I tell this to my people in my preaching; that there is another place to which a white man goes. He goes up all right, but must be to another part."

55. AN EXPERIENCE OF DICK BENSON[220]

My uncle, Dick Benson, died. He was a [reservation] policeman. He was wicked; he left his wife for another woman. They laid him out when he died. Some boys drummed and prayed for him. Smoke came out of his body.

They [heaven's denizens] told him he would have to return to earth because he had drunk, gambled, etc. "You will have to go back and pray every day.

Then you can get through."

He lay dead all day, but he came back to life. He confessed and told his people not to gamble, nor drink, nor to steal lovers.

"You have to be of proper mind to go through when you die." All his children heeded him for a while. He lived through the year until the next spring when he died. This was when I [Mrs. Teio] was a little girl [ca. 1860-65.]

56. A GRAND RONDE WOMAN'S VISION
BEYOND THE BORDER[221]

[McWhorter's notes: During [the] winter of 1924-25 an aged woman of the Grand Ronde [band] became very ill, and a noted medicine woman of the Yakimas was in attendance. Sinking day by day, she at last told those about her]:

"Something seems not right. Should I die, do not bury me after the customary time has elapsed, but hold my body until the third day. At noon, if I am still dead, then bury me."

She also directed that she not be wrapped in blankets after the usual custom.

Sometime after that the sick woman apparently died; and as directed she was not bundled ready for burial as usual, but left unsmothered by blankets. On the second day some [neighbors] started to bury her, but the medicine woman would not allow it. Sometime during the forenoon of the third day, it was observed that the toes of one of her feet slightly moved, and within a short time she requested to be raised up. Taking hold of a string of wampum beads about her neck, she said: "Take this off."

Her request was complied with.

A fine shawl was next ordered removed; and when this was done, she explained: "I was met on the Trail and told that I must return and leave these things, for they had been stolen; that I could not enter the Better Land unless I did this. With these stolen bad things I would have to remain on the Trail forever."

It developed that this woman's daughter had stolen the articles, all unknown to the mother. The woman was still living when this story [statement] was given me [McWhorter], in March 1925, but she was described as extremely emaciated and extremely weak.

57. DREAM VISION OF A RENEGADE[222]

[McWhorter notes: A medicine man of the *Yakimas*, with whom I am well acquainted, had this dream-vision while suffering from indisposition]:

It was several years ago that I was unwell and went on the spirit trail. I came where I saw some of my old-time friends who had passed before. It was in the *Cowiche*, not far from here. I saw my people, and I knew them. I tried to go to them, but a man stopped me. He held an Indian flute in his left hand, a flute made from a bloody gun. His arms were blood to the elbow. I attempted to pass him, but he held me back, bared my way with the gun.

He said: "You can not come here now. See my hands? They are yours, all blood and bad. Go back to where you came from! Clean the blood from your hands and arms. Do good for your people. Live right!

When you have done this, you may come to this place, but not before. Go back! Make a tea-medicine from the young growing willows. Drink it for five days. Make medicine from the elder and drink it during five days. Do this, and you will become well and live many years."

Then I came back to life and made the medicines as directed. I drank it as instructed, and became well and strong. I am now getting old, but I have tried to do good for my people whenever I could.

[McWhorter notes: From that time there was a marked reformation in the life of this Indian. The symbol of the bloody gun and hands he attributed to the following episode in his earlier life:]

Of a reckless and daring disposition, he joined a band of four white horse thieves. Their first venture was rounding up a bunch of horses in Oregon and driving them into Idaho, where they were disposed of. Then, from the Idaho range they secured another band, drove them back to Oregon, and successfully converted the animals into cash. A third holding, made up in that state, was bartered at Spokane Falls. A fourth band, taken from Washington, was moved into Idaho and "turned" without trouble.

The five men now rode back to Washington, where the two recognized leaders, in a quarrel, were killed in the pistol duel which followed. The Indian with his two remaining white companions drifted back to his home, the Yakima Reservation. Camping for a few days just below Union Gap, the white men came on to Yakima City, where they obtained a supply of whiskey.

Next day the party struck tent and proceeded

south, crossing the Toppenish-Satus Mountain, where they camped in the timber. The white men, stupid with drink, ordered the Indian to prepare supper; and, dropping on their blankets with six-shooters in hand, were soon in drunken slumber. The Indian, although unacquainted with the culinary art, complied, and when the "bannocks" and coffee were ready, he proceeded to rouse his companions.

Shaking one of them with his foot, he said: "Here! Here! Grub! Get up!"

This was repeated with the second man, who protested in threatening language. Returning to the other man who had again dozed off, he gave him another prod with his toe, ordering him up. Both men now raised on their elbows and bringing their guns up, swore that they would kill him. Alert, and ever wary of treachery, the Indian leaped aside with a gun in either hand. One of the men fell back dead, and the other was killed as he gained his feet. Both their shots had failed to score.

Rifling the bodies of money belts, the Indian dragged them into the brush and concealed them. In the outfit were two or three extra saddles. And these, with those of the dead men, he hung high among the branches of some evergreens. He then proceeded with the horses to Warm Springs, Oregon. With a companion from that tribe, whom I [McWhorter] well knew, he soon spent the money obtained in crime, most of it in Portland. Two years later, completely broke, he returned to the scene of tragedy on the Satus; and with the help of another tribesman, recovered the *cache* of saddles. The skeletons of the victims were found with boots and fragments of clothing still adhering.

58. A BORDER VISION[223]

[Mcwhorter notes:] "A young Yakima woman who had been reared a Catholic, joined the Shaker Church. In her last illness, she "died" and then came back to life."

Deeply affected, she called her father and said: "My father! I will go soon. I did very wrong to join the Shakers. While away, I saw a filthy, greasy table. I was seated there, and they brought me cooked *Wah'k-puch* on a plate. It was for me to eat."[224] "I do not want to die this way. Hurry! Go quickly for the priest. Bring him here! Let me take the Sacrament! Let him bless me, that I may die holy. Hurry, my father, for I have not long to stay with you."

The father, who is well known to me [McWhorter], hastily procured the priest; and, shriven, the dying woman passed wholly comforted.

59. THE VISION OF *IN-WAT-KEE* OF THE WISHOMS[225]

[Narrated by her daughter, *Sin-i-tah*]: My mother was not a medicine woman, but she often cured or helped the sick. Her power came through many uncles and cousins. But she herself became sick, was sick much of the time. The medicine man took her illness from her and threw it away. But before this, she was ill quite a while, grew sicker and weaker. Sometimes she would die for three or four hours at a time, but always returned to life again.

Just before the last of such experiences, she

said to us: "If I die that way again, do not bury me soon. Let me lay in the house at least two days. Then, if I am still dead, you can bury me."

I was then a young girl. You see that I am now growing old. It was not long until mother died again. We left her five hours without disturbing her. Not returning to life, we bathed and dressed her, and laid her on a couch of blankets. It was in the morning when mother died; and all that day, all the night she lay dead. The next day, when most of the afternoon was gone, my mother came back to life. I was there, and I saw it all.

Mother spoke to us. She said: "Clean outside the house. Clean inside the house."

We did this, cleaned everything as mother directed. Then she called the people together and told them a story of what she had found. I heard my mother talking, and I remember her words. She said: "It was just as though I was traveling in this country; but I knew not where I was going. I went quite a ways on a small trail, when I heard the voice of some person talking. I kept going. I saw a man sitting on the ground. He was to the left of the trail; sitting in ashes; all dirty; no clothes, naked. I stopped, stood on the trail, looking. I did not go up close, but I could see him. I knew him; a big Chief who had died. He was talking. I heard his words, what he was saying. He talked of how rich he was, what property he had: horses, blankets and other things. He would like to have more property, become richer still. He would like to cheat poor people; he wanted to get all that he could. He was talking like that, saying bad things."

"I heard the voices of two women answering

the chief, answering all that he said; but I could not see them. I knew the voices of those women, know the women themselves. They are not yet dead. They were his two wives who are here now listening to my talk.

"I left the naked Chief sitting there, dirty; scratching in the ashes with a stick; talking how he wanted more riches. I heard a voice back of me say: "Chief _____ will get no farther on the trail to the happy land. He will stay here always, just as you see him, clothes worn out. Naked, dirty; he is always wanting riches. Not far on the trail had he gone until he grew tired; longing for riches as when [he was] on earth. A big man, he will get no farther."

I kept on the trail. I heard a noise, a singing as they came to meet me. A boy met me, not on the trail but as if flying.

He said: "My aunt! I want to talk to you a little."

I stopped.

He spoke again: "Do you not know me?"

I answered: "No! I do not know you."

He said: "I am the Chief's grandson. It was my grandfather you saw back there on the trail. You are going but a short ways now. When you go back, tell my mother what I am saying to you. She must arise on *Sapalwit* [Sunday] morning and sweep the house. Sweep all outside. Sweep clean after she has started a fire. When finished, she must come in the house. Make herself clean; comb her hair; put on a clean dress. The first food that she cooks must be *salmon*, then *bitterroot* and all Indian foods. When she places this food on the matting, she must pray; must sing the song which I will give you. Before eating, she must first take water. Next take salmon, then the other Indian foods."

"My mother must not bite the people with bitter words as she has been doing. When she quarrels with them, she bites them. She must not do this any more."

"The same way with my father, both he and mother. They must not do these things. They want to be rich; my father wants to be Head Chief. They are doing a bad thing, must not continue on that trail."

The boy then gave me this song for his mother to sing when placing the food on the matting:

"The time the sun went travelling,
He turned himself to the right.
The sun went farther up;
The salmon grew bright, Just like the sun;
For our bodies."

Then the boy disappeared.

He had said to me: "Keep going! You will see something after awhile."

I continued traveling. I heard a noise, someone talking as I had heard [near] the naked Chief. But it was from another man. I came up. There was Chief _____ who had died several snows before. Naked! Dirty! He sat in ashes, stirring them with a stick as had the other Chief. He talked the same thing, the same way. A big-bodied man, he wanted more horses; grabbing from poor people always. I stopped for only a little while, then kept going.

I came to wild currants, yellow and ripe. I saw chokecherries, all close along the trail. I did not stop, did not touch them. I had heard that if you eat on the trail to the spirit world, you do not get there. I kept going. I came to huckleberries, lots of them. It is a fine country; everything large and nice. I passed all these things, keeping on the trail. Then I heard voices again, coming to meet me. They came! My own son and the son of *Spe-hi*; a good woman, and aunt to the first boy who met me. They talked to me same as the other boy had, some word for *Spe-hi* to do certain things each *Sapalwit*.

Then my own boy said to me: "My mother! To you from a girl [since girlhood] bringing you up, have come many bad things. You have been thinking of doing some good deeds. You thought they were good, but they were not. You will have to go back over the trail. You will have to stay till you grow old. Work every *Sapalwit* at what I am telling you. Make yourself clean. You must not forget any of the things I am telling you. You will have to do them all before you can reach this place."

After telling me what I must do, he gave me these two songs:

> (1) "I did tell my mother,
> >   You never see us children.
> >   [Repeated several times]

> (2) "My dear mother!
> >   You are the only one
> >   Who has the record
> And the word.
> >   You are not clear
> >   of Sin as I am."

Then the boys waved their hands upward. I looked! I saw a nice green country. I saw many people, all dressed alike; clean and happy. Trees and water were there; all fine. The two boys disappeared.

After a short time I thought: "I will go home."

I turned about on the trail, and found myself here in this house. I am to stay for a time, and must do the things as directed before I can go to the fine place that I have seen.

In-wat-kee lived twenty years after this experience, and up to her death she sacredly observed the rules and life regulations given her in vision by her departed son. One of the deceased chief's, whose spirit is described as earth-bound, was an historic character, a branch of whose family is prominent in present day tribal affairs.

60. VISION OF *QUAS-QUI TA'CHENS*[226]

[McWhorter notes]:   *Ta'chens*, who died of lung trouble, belonged to the Yakimas. His death came in the evening. The body was bathed, dressed and blanketed, all made ready for burial. The next morning life returned, and he sat up. Many persons were in the room; the long-lodge where dwelt several families. They saw, but spoke not a word."

For several moments *Ta'chens* said nothing; then he asked for *chuch* (water). Tears ran down his cheeks.

After a time he spoke: "Come about me, my friends! I must tell you why I have come back. I will tell you what I have seen and heard."

"I went up to the good world, but the great man said to me: 'You must go back and pure [purify] yourself of all wrong before coming here. Go back! Tell your people of the wrong things you have done. Instruct them how to live, how to do right! Do this! Then you may come to this happy place.'"

"I did not see the 'great man,' only heard the voice. I saw no one; only heard. Then I received instructions to give you, but I must first tell of my wrongs.

"I have done bad things. I used to beat my wife because she did not always attend the children when they were crying. She might be busy at work. I thought that she should stop and care for them. I would strike her with a stick or anything I might have in my hand. Blood would run from big cuts in her head where I struck her. This now hurts me more than any thing else. *An-a-whoa* is a good woman. I did wrong to strike her. She is the same as my mother. All women are as our mothers, which I did not know until now.

"I have done many bad things as I now see them. I have not been true to *An-a-whoa*. Evil enters the home in this way. Shadows are cast which never leave us.

"My friends! I will soon go again, not to return. Listen to my words! I see three here whom I saw on the trail, who will be first to follow me. But there is something before you, something in your way. Your lives are not right. You will not travel to the good place unless you change. I am telling you this, as it passed before me in the other land."

These men died very soon afterwards as predicted. They wept when *Ta'chens* foretold their fate.

Ta'chens lived three days and then died. During this interval, he constantly talked to his friends, instructing them in worship and how to lead better lives. Among other things, he gave them a word-ceremony to be used before partaking of food. This rite is supposed to be observed every day, but in general it is in evidence only on *Sapalwit*, or Sunday. Like revelations of a kindred nature, this of *Ta'chens* was largely directed to his immediate relatives and friends. The word-ceremony, used as a chant, follows:

"We must not be like our mothers—
As they used to be.[227]
We must be careful what we do!
We must be like the little chil dren.
Little children were blessed by Him.
Like the little children; and
Now they are up with Him forever!"

In his vision *Ta'chens* heard, as his spirit was leaving the body, a mystery voice singing:

"Now be careful!
Where you are stepping!
Step on the back of the little bird.
It will bring [you] up to this new world.
Which you have never seen before.
Then you will be rejoiced over."

This chant in use is repeated in song three times. *Ta'chens* had never been known to speak of these stanzas prior to his vision. For three days he enlightened his family and friends on how to live better lives, that they might obtain a happy future.

At the end of that time he said to those about him: "Goodby! I am going to a good place. I will not return." Then chanting the stanzas which he had given them, and as all lifted the right hand at the conclusion in the accustomed, fervent "*A-a-a-yi!*" *Ta'chens* fell back on his couch, dead.

Ta'chens stated that when in vision he was leaving his body, the voice of the unseen singer admonished him and instructed him how to depart. He was told to step upon the back of a small bird, to him invisible. When he did this, he was borne upwards through space. Arriving at the entrance to the better world, he was ordered back as narrated.[228]

Ta'chens was not a Christian, had never received Christian training. He could not speak the English tongue. He believed in the old Indian religion, and was versed in the wisdom [lore] of his race.

INDEX OF MOTIFS

To underscore the traditionality of the death vision narratives, their *motifs* have been noted hereafter. By *motif* we mean that "... smallest element in a tale having a power to persist in tradition. . . . Most motifs fall into three classes. First are actors in a tale. . .; second come certain items in the background of the action, magic object, unusual customs, strange beliefs, and the like. . .; in the third place there are single incidents—and these comprise the great majority of motifs" Thompson, Stith 1946. *The Folktale*, New York: The Dryden Press, p. 415. We have employed Thompson's *Motif-index of folk-literature*, six vols., here.

50. DREAM PRESENTMENT OF DEATH

C. Tabu

C401.1.	Tabu: speaking during vigil [respect for dead]

D. Magic

D1731.2.	Marvels seen in dreams [visions]
D1810.8.2.	Information received through dream
D1812.3.3.	Future revealed in dream
D1814.2.	Advice from dream
D1825.7.1.	Person sees phantom procession before funeral actually takes place
D1825.7.1.1.	Band of the dead do not look in passing at he/she next to die

E. The Dead

E491.	Procession of the dead [the dead passabout house]
E720.1.	Souls of human beings seen in dream
E722.2.9.	Dead friends come for dying person's soul [in vision]

F. Marvels

F655.3.	Person beholding dead and death parade is nearly blind
F1041.9.4.	Extraordinary [lengthy/grave] illness [assoc. with vision]

V. Religion

V68.2.2.	Preparations for death: bathe, put on clean clothes, clean house, etc.; cf. V412.3.
V510.	Religious visions

W. Traits of Character
- W230.1.   A son-in-law
- W230.2.1.   A daughter
- W230.2.1.   Woman [Black Bear] as narrator/primary character in tale
- W230.4.   Many [dead] people [entire band seen]

Z. Miscellaneous Groups of Motifs
- Z71.1.   Three [vision recounted 3 days before death] [person dead 3 days after] [dead pass by 3 times]
- Z71.2.1.3.   East-direction [east window]

51. VISION OF AN AGED
WARM SPRINGS WOMAN

A. Mythological Motifs
- A310.   God of heaven [Great Man Personage—not seen, only heard]

C. Tabu
- C542.1.1.   Tabu: contact with things on journey to heaven: [Deceased aren't permitted to recognize {speak to} their children]

D. Magic
- D1275.   Magic song ["word ceremony"]
- D1825.3.3.3. Person sees the familiar dead [deceased children]

E. The Dead
- E391.   Woman dies but returns to life—tells of journey to land of dead
- E720.1.1.   Deceased children seen in vision: meet mother on trail

F. Marvels
- F57.1.   Narrow road [trail?] to heaven

Q. Rewards and Punishments
- Q520.7.2.   Unrequited sins bar one's entrance to heaven [speaking with deceased children]

V. Religion
- V510.   Religious visions

W. Traits of Character

W230.1.1.1.	Unknown speaker
W230.2.1.	An old woman

52. VISION OF _____

A. Mythological Motifs

A661.	Heaven: A blissful Upper World
A661.3.1.	Heaven, lush country containing bushes heavy with ripe berries, forests with fish
A671.	Hell: lower world of torment ["wild yells, screaming, sounds of fighting"]

B. Animals

B11.3.6.1.	Snakes, rattlesnakes, and frogs in lower world
B17.1.2.	Great dog (hound)
B611.2.	Dog paramour; cf. B601.2. Marriage to dog

D. Magic

D1731.2.	Marvels seen in dreams [visions]
D1810.8.2.	Information received through dream
D1812.3.3.	Future revealed in dream
D1812.5.1.2.	Bad dream as evil omen
D1814.2.	Advice from dream
D1814.3.	Advice from God (or gods); cf. a speaker

E. The Dead

E391.	Dead returns to life and tells of journey to land of dead
E481.2.3.	A straight [walking] trail extends to heaven
E481.4.	Beautiful land of the dead
E720.1.	Souls of human beings seen [heard only] in dream
E721.	Soul journeys from the body [after a short time, returns]
E721.2.	Body in trance while soul is absent
E721.7.	Soul leaves body to visit [region of] Hell (Heaven)
E755.1.	Souls in heaven

F. Marvels

F11.	Journey to heaven (upper-world paradise)
F57.1.	Narrow road [trail?] to heaven; cf. F171.2.
F81.	Descent to lower world of dead [Hell, Hades]
F167.3.1.	Giant in lower world; cf. N111.5. Giant as clerk to God of Destiny; cf. also A133.3
F1041.9.5.	Extraordinary [grave] accident assoc. with vision

G. Ogres
  G20.2.   Ghouls in otherworld: gnaw on bones, devour human flesh

M. Ordaining the Future
  M302.7.   Prophecy through dreams

P. Society
  P716.   Particular Upper World Death Place: "Happy Land;" "Better Spirit Land"

Q. Rewards and Punishments
  Q172.10.   Woman admitted to trail to heaven upon learning *correct* path; cf. F150.1. Way to otherworld hard to find
  Q520.7.   Unrequited sins bar one's entrance to heaven
  Q522.9.   Penance: gambling for release from hell
  Q560.   Punishments in hell
  Q565.   Man/Woman admitted to neither heaven nor hell

V. Religion
  V510.   Religious visions
  V511.2.   Visions of hell
  V522.   Sinner reformed after visit to heaven and hell [in this narrative sinner falls away again]

W. Traits of Character
  W230.1.   A young man
  W230.1.1.   King of the Underworld
  W230.1.1.1.   Unknown speaker [directs departed souls on upper trail]
  W230.2.1.   Women met on trail [white woman] [black woman] [1-Indian woman, 2-Indian woman]

Z. Miscellaneous Groups of Motifs
  Z71.0.3.   Enumeration of wrongs in life
  Z127.3.1.   Lust Personified [white woman/black woman met on trail]; cf. T336. Sight or touch of woman as source of sin
  Z127.4.   Irreligiosity Personified [lush berry bushes, roots beside trail reflect failure to observe religious feasts]
  Z127.5.   Gambling personified [giant as croupier in hell]

53. VISION OF *I-KEEP-SWAH*
(SITTING ROCK)

A. Mythological Motifs

A671.	Hell: lower world of torment [earth as transformed to hell]
A671.0.2.1.	Fire in hell [fire covers all the earth]

D. Magic

D1810.8.2.	Information received through dream
D1812.3.3.	Future revealed in dream [death in 8 years]
D1812.5.1.2.	Bad dream as evil omen
D1814.2.	Advice from dream
D1814.3.	Advice from God (or gods); cf. Speaker

E. The Dead

E391.	Dead returns to life and tells of journey to land of dead
E481.4.	Land of dead—up in sky; cf A661
E721.	Soul journeys from the body [returns after a short time]
E721.2.	Body in trance while soul is absent
E721.7.	Soul leaves body to visit region of hell (or heaven)

F. Marvels

F11.	Journey to heaven (upperworld paradise)
F821.6.	Shroud-like covering covers entire body
F1041.9.5.	Extraordinary [grave] accident assoc. with vision
F1068.1.1.	Advice and information given in dream [concerning others in life]

H. Tests

H51.2.	Scar as mark of veracity of teller

M. Ordaining the Future

M302.7.	Prophecy through dreams [concerning self, also sinful world]
M341.1.5.3.	Prophecy: death within eight years
M359.11.	Prophecy: in nine years [ten years] earth will grow hot and shake [quake?]

Q. Rewards and Punishments

Q520.7.	Unrequited sins bar one's entrance to heaven
Q565.	Man admitted to neither heaven nor hell

V. Religion

V510.	Religious visions
V511.2.	Visions of hell [of earth become as hell]
V522.	Sinner reformed after visit to heaven and/or hell
V543.	Interpretative Voice: orders sinner to reform, stop drinking, "doctoring," etc.; cf. R341. Escape by intervention of Providence

W. Traits of Character

W230.1.	Young man [*I-keeps-Swah*]
W230.1.1.1.	Unknown speaker [on upper trail, directs departed souls]

Z. Miscellaneous Groups of Motifs

Z71.2.2.5.	Travel upward
Z71.0.3.	Enumeration of wrongs in life
Z71.6.	Nine
Z71.16.2.	Ten
Z71.16.8.	Eight

54. VISION OF CHARLEY _____

A. Mythological Motifs

A661.	Heaven: a blissful upper world [Indians only, no whites] {whites go elsewhere}
A661.3.1.	Heaven, a lush country containing bushes heavy with ripe berries, forests with fish and game

C. Tabu

C542.1.1.	Tabu: contact with things on journey to heaven [don't pick, don't touch, etc.]

D. Magic

D1275.	Magic song; also D1275. Magic music, etc.; cf. D1601.18.0.1. Magic musical instrument reproduces songs sung in heaven
D1731.2.	Marvels seen in dreams [visions]
D1791.	Magic power by circumambulation-"rightwise"; cf. D1384.3.1.; also cf. N131.2.
D1810.8.2.	Information received through dream ["wicked, you must go back, live right"]
D1814.2.	Advice from dream ["go back, live right"]
D1814.3.	Advice from God (or gods); cf. Speaker
1825.3.3.3.	Person sees the familiar dead [mother, spouse, etc.] during vision [dead refuse to talk to him]

E. The Dead

E391.	Dead returns to life and tells of journey to land of dead
E480.	Abode of the dead
E481.4.	Beautiful land of dead
E481.4.1.	Land of the dead—up in sky; cf. A661.
E720.1.	Souls of human beings seen in dream [mother, etc.]
E721.	Soul journeys from the body [returns after a short time]
E721.2.	Body in trance while soul is absent
E721.7.	Soul leaves body to visit region of hell (or heaven)
E755.1.	Souls in heaven [only a glimpse]

F. Marvels

F11.	Journey to heaven (upperworld paradise)
F1068.1.	Advice and information given in dream [concerning others in life]

M. Ordaining the Future

M302.7.	Prophecy through dreams

Q. Rewards and Punishments

Q520.7.	Unrequited sins bar one's one's entrance to heaven
Q522.9.1.	Pennance: teach magic song to the living
Q565.	Man admitted to neither heaven nor hell

V. Religion

V510.	Religious visions
V511.1.	Visions of heaven
V522.	Sinner reformed after visit to heaven and hell
V543.	Interpretive Voice: orders sinner to reform, stop drinking, "doctoring," etc.; cf. R341. Escape by intervention of Providence

W. Traits of Character

W230.1.	A man [Charley _____]
W230.1.1.1.	Unknown speaker [on upper trail departed dead seen] {wearing buckskins, decorated with eagle feathers, yellow paint}

Z. Miscellaneous Groups of Motifs

Z71.1.	Three ["dead" 3 days]
Z71.2.2.5.	Travel upward

55. AN EXPERIENCE OF DICK BENSON

D. Magic

D1810.8.2.	Information received through dream
D1812.3.3.	Future revealed in dream
D1814.2.	Advice from dream [go back—live right]
D1814.3.	Advice from God (or gods); cf. Speaker

E. The Dead

E391.	Dead returns to life and tells of journey to land of dead
E721.	Soul journeys from the body [returns after a short time]
E721.2.	Body in trance while soul is absent
E721.7.	Soul leaves body to visit region of hell (or heaven)
E743.1.	Soul [of bad man] as smoke; cf. G303.17.2.1. Devil, detected, goes up chimney in smoke
E754.2.	Saved soul goes to heaven [upon doing pennance, he'll "get through"]

F. Marvels

F11.	Journey to heaven (upperworld paradise)
F1068.1.1.	Advice and information given in dream [concerning others in life]

M. Ordaining the Future

M302.7.	Prophecy through dreams

Q. Rewards and Punishments

Q172.	Reward: admission to heaven [upon doing pennance, he'll "get through"]
Q520.7.	Unrequited sins bar one's entrance to heaven
Q522.9.2.	Pennance: "to confess—tell the people not to gamble, drink nor steal lovers"
Q565.	Man admitted to neither heaven nor hell

V. Religion

V510.	Religious visions
V511.1.	Visions of heaven
V522.	Sinner reformed after visit to heaven and/or hell
V543.	Interpretive Voice: orders sinner to reform, stop drinking, "doctoring," etc.; cf. R341. Escape by intervention of Providence

W. Traits of Character

W230.1.   A man [Dick Benson]

W230.1.1.1.   Unknown speaker [on upper trail directs departed dead]

Z. Miscellaneous Groups of Motifs

Z71.0.3.   Enumeration of wrongs in life

Z71.0.0.   One [lay dead 1 day]

56. A GRAND RONDE WOMAN'S VISION BEYOND THE BORDER

D. Magic

D1810.8.2.   Information received through dream

D1812.3.3.   Future revealed in dream

D1814.2.   Advice from dream

D1814.3.   Advice from God (or gods); cf. Speaker

E. The Dead

E391.   Dead returns to life and tells of journey to land of dead

E481.2.3.   A straight [walking] trail extends to heaven

E721.   Soul journeys from the body [returns after a short time]

E721.2.   Body in trance while soul is absent

E721.7.   Soul leaves body to visit region of hell (or heaven)

E754.2.   Saved soul goes to heaven [only by returning stolen items can
               woman enter Better Land]

F. Marvels

F57.1.   Narrow road [trail?] to heaven; cf. F171.2.

F1041.9.4.   Extraordinary [grave] illness assoc. with vision

F1068.1.1.   Advice and information given in dream [concerning others
               in life]

M. Ordaining the Future

M302.7.   Prophecy through dreams

P. Society

P683.1.   Burial customs: delay of interment for 3 days

P683.2.   Burial customs: delay wrapping corpse in blankets

P716.   Particular Upper World Place: "Better Land"

Q. Rewards and Punishments

Q172.   Reward: admission to heaven [upon returning stolen items]

Q520.7.   Unrequited sins bar one's entrance to heaven

Q522.9.3.   Pennance: return of stolen items: beads, a shawl

Q565.   Man admitted to neither heaven nor hell

V. Religion

V510.   Religious visions

V522.   Sinner reformed after visit to heaven and/or hell

V543.   Interpretive Voice: orders sinner to reform, stop drinking, "doctoring," etc.; cf. R341. Escape by intervention of Providence

W. Traits of Character

W230.1.1.1.   Unknown speaker [on upper trail directs departed souls]

W230.2.1.   An old woman

Z. Miscellaneous Groups of Motifs

Z71.0.3.   Enumeration of wrongs in life

Z71.1.   Three [buried after 3 days][revives on 3d day]["dead" 3 days]

57. DREAM VISION OF A RENEGADE

D. Magic

D1223.1.1.   Magic Indian flute

D1731.2.   Marvels seen in dreams [visions]

D1810.8.2.   Information received through dream

D1812.3.3.   Future revealed in dream [to live many years]

D1814.2.   Advice from dream

D1814.3.   Advice from God (or gods); cf. Speaker

D1825.3.3.3.   Persons sees the familiar dead [friends, etc.]

E. The Dead

E391.   Dead returns to life and tells of journey to land of dead

E720.1.   Souls of human beings seen in dream

E721.   Soul journeys from the body [returns after a short time]

E721.2.   Body in trance while soul is absent

E721.7.   Soul leaves body to visit region of hell (or heaven)

F. Marvels

F11.   Journey to heaven upperworld paradise)

F1041.9.4.   Extraordinary [grave/lengthy] illness [assoc. with vision]

F1068.1.1.   Advice and information given in dream [concerning others in life]

M. Ordaining the Future
    M302.7.   Prophecy through dreams

P. Society
    P716.   Particular Death Place: ["in the Cowiche"]

Q. Rewards and Punishments
    Q172.   Reward: admission to heaven [upon taking tea {self-purification?}]
    Q520.7.   Unrequited sins bar one's entrance to heaven [murders]
    Q522.9.4.   Pennance: make tea medicines [from elderberry, willows] cleanse self, do good for the Indian people
    Q565.   Man admitted to neither heaven nor hell

V. Religion
    V510.   Religious visions
    V522.   Sinner reformed after visit to heaven and/or hell
    V543.   Interpretive Voice: orders sinner to reform, stop drinking, "doctoring," etc.; cf. R341. Escape by intervention of Providence

W. Traits of Character
    W230.1.   Young man
    W230.1.1.   Several young men
    W230.1.1.1.   Unknown speaker [on upper trail, directs *departed souls*]

Z. Miscellaneous Groups of Motifs
    Z71.0.3.   Enumeration of wrongs in life [alludes to murders done]
    Z127.6.   Multiple murders exemplified in *Indian flute*: "made from a bloody gun," with bloody arms of the unknown speaker

58. A BORDER VISION

D. Magic
    D1731.2.   Marvels seen in dreams [visions]
    D1810.8.2.   Information received through dream
    D1812.3.3.   Future revealed in dream
    D1812.5.1.2.   Bad dream as evil omen
    D1814.2.   Advice from dream

E. The Dead
    E391.   Dead returns to life and tells of journey to land of dead

| E721. | Soul journeys from the body [returns after a short time] |
| E721.7. | Soul leaves body to visit region of hell (or heaven) |

F. Marvels

| F1041.9.4. | Extraordinary [grave] [lengthy] illness [assoc. with vision] |

M. Ordaining the Future

| M302.7. | Prophecy through dreams |
| M359.12. | Prophetic vision: Shaker heaven like a filthy, greasy table at which is served cooked rattlesnake |

Q. Rewards and Punishments

Q520.7.	Unrequited sins bar one's entrance to heaven [sin of apostasy]
Q522.9.5.	Pennance: take last rites of Roman Catholic church [undo apostasy]
Q565.	Person admitted to neither heaven nor hell

V. Religion

V68.2.2.	Preparations for death: specific prerequisites [be shrived by priest]
V337.	Conversion from Roman Catholicism to the Shaker faith
V510.	Religious visions
V522.	Sinner reformed after visit to heaven and/or hell

Z. Miscellaneous Groups of Motifs

| Z71.2. | A young woman |

59. THE VISION OF *IN-WAT-KEE*
OF THE WISHOMS

A. Mythological Motifs

| A661. | Heaven: a blissful upper world |
| A661.3.1. | Heaven: a lush country containing bushes heavy with ripe berries; forests with fish and game |

C. Tabu

| C542.1.1. | Tabu: contact with things on journey to heaven [don't pick and eat berries, etc.] |

D. Magic

| D1275. | Magic Song; also D1275. Magic music, etc.; cf. D1601.18.0.1. Magic musical instrument reproduces songs sung in heaven |

[two separate incidents of magic song]

D1711.	Medicine man (shaman)
D1721.0.2.1.	Magic power received through uncles and cousins
D1731.2.	Marvels seen in dreams dreams [visions]
D1791.	Magic power by ambulation; but more: see D1791.2. Withershins (countersunwise) circuit [to the left] (for ill luck); cf. esp. C643. Tabu: Turning left side of chariot toward certain place
D1810.8.2.	Information received through dream
D1812.3.3.	Future revealed in dream [must stay on earth, do pennance]
D1812.5.1.2.	Bad dream as evil omen
D1813.1.6.	Dream shows others in danger
D1814.2.	Advice from dream
D1814.3.	Advice from God (or gods); cf. Speaker
D1825.3.3.3.	Person sees the familiar dead [familiar acquaintances, other's kin]
D2161.4.2.5.	Illness taken from patient and *thrown away*

E. The Dead

E391.	Dead returns to life and tells of journey to land of dead
E480.	Abode of the dead ["like this country"]
E481.2.3.	A straight [walking] trail extends to heaven
E481.4.	Beautiful land of dead [glimpse of heaven]
E481.4.1.	Land of dead—up in sky
E720.1.	Souls of human beings seen in dream
E721.	Soul journeys from the body [returns after a short time]
E721.2.	Body in trance while soul is absent
E721.7.	Soul leaves body to visit region of hell (or heaven) [travels only half-way on trail]

F. Marvels

F57.1.	Narrow road [trail?] to heaven ["on a small trail"]
F1041.9.4.	Extraordinary [grave/lengthy] illness [assoc. with vision]
F1068.1.1.	Advice and information given in dream [concerning others in life] {esp. listeners to live better lives—upon hearing of their kin in death}

M. Ordaining the Future

M302.7.	Prophecy through dreams

P. Society

P683.1.	Burial customs: delay of interment [for 2 days]

Q. Rewards and Punishments

Q520.7. Unrequited sins bar one's entrance to heaven [the several personifications/ needed pennance]

Q522.9.1. Pennance: teach magic song to the living

Q522.9.6. Pennance: make self clean, perform particulars on *Sapalwit*, learn-teach two songs

Q522.9.7. Pennance for mother (and father): 1-Observe *Sapalwit* (clean person, house, foods) 2-not be bitterly quarrelsome; 3-cease pursuit of wealth; 4-learn and sing *Sapalwit song*

Q565. Person admitted to neither heaven nor hell [turned back]

V. Religion

V68.2.2. Preparations for death: Specific prequisites [clean house: outside/inside]

V231.7. Youth flies [like an angel]; cf. V230.1. Woman beholds angels

V510. Religious visions

V511.1. Visions of heaven [a brief glimpse]

V522. Sinner reformed after visit to heaven and/or hell

V543. Interpretive Voice: orders sinner to reform, stop drinking, "doctoring," etc.; cf. R341. Escape by intervention of Providence

W. Traits of Character

W230. An old woman *In-wat-kee* [as related by her daughter]

W230.1.1.1. Unknown speaker [on upper trail, directs "departed souls"]

Z. Miscellaneous Groups of Motifs

Z71.0. Two [lay unburied 2 days]

Z71.1. Three [dies 3 or 4 days at a time—revives]

Z71.3. Five [5 hours corpse left undisturbed]

Z127.7. Personification of Ill-gotten Riches [a rich man—dirty, sitting in ashes, naked, discoursing on how to gain more wealth by cheating poor people]

Z127.8. Personification of Ill-gotten Riches [a rich man, dirty, sitting in ashes, discoursing on how to gain more wealth [horses] "grabbing from the poor people."

60. VISION OF *QUAS-QUI TA'CHENS*

A. Mythological Motifs

A211. God of heaven [Great Man- not seen, only heard]

A310. God of the world of the dead [Great Man]

B. Animals
B39.2.   Mythical small bird carries the dead upward to the "better world"; cf. E754.2.1.

C. Tabu
C401.1.   Tabu: speaking during vigil [respect for the dead]

D. Magic
D996.   Right hand-[lifted at end of chant]; cf.

D996.1.1.   Magic power of right hand for good; cf. N113.2.1. Lucky right hand; cf.V52.15.

D1275.   Magic Song ["word cere-mony"]; also D1275 Magicmusic, etc.; cf. D1601.18.0.1. Magic musical instrument reproduces songs sung in heaven

D1810.8.2.   Information received through dream [too wicked-go back, live right]

D1814.2.   Advice from dream

D1814.3.   Advice from god (or gods); cf. Speaker

E. The Dead
E391.   Dead returns to life and tells of journey to land of dead

E481.4.1.   Land of dead—up in sky [cf. A661] ["good world"]

E721.   Soul journeys from the body [returns after a short time]

E721.2.   Body in trance while soul is absent

E721.7.   Soul leaves body to visit region of hell (or heaven) [only travels half-way on trail]

E754.2.0.1.   Dead carried upward to heaven on back of small bird

F. Marvels
F1041.9.4.   Extraordinary [grave/lengthy] illness [assoc. with vision]

F1068.1.1.   Advice and information given in dream [concerning others in life]

M. Ordaining the Future
M341.1.5.3.   Death of three men to occur in short time

M359.11.   Prophecy: Unless three men change their lives, they will go to hell; cf. Q560. Punishment in hell

P. Society
P716.   Particular Death Place: "good world"

Q. Rewards and Punishments

Q520.7.   Unrequited sins bar one's entrance to heaven

Q522.9.1.   Pennance: Teach magic song ["word ceremony"] to the living

Q522.9.7.   Pennance: To confess wrongs—wife-beating, adultery

Q522.9.8.   Pennance: Do good to people—1) instruct them in worship, how to lead better lives; 2) teach a "word-ceremony [chant]" for use before meals

Q565.   Man admitted to neither heaven nor hell [turned back "on the trail"]

V. Religion

V510.   Religious visions

V522.   Sinner reformed after visit to heaven and/or hell

V543.   Interpretive Voice: orders sinner to reform, stop drinking, "doctoring," etc.[voice of "Great Man"]; cf. R341. Escape by intervention of Providence

W. Traits of Character

W230.1.1.   A man-*Ta'chens*

W230.1.1.1.   Unknown speaker ["Great Man"]

Z. Miscellaneous Groups of Motifs

Z71.1.   Three [chant repeated 3 times]

Z71.2.2.5.   Travel upward

NOTES TO THE NARRATIVES

PART ONE

PREFACE

1. Park, W.Z. 1938. *Shamanism in Western North America: A Study in Cultural Relationships,* NUSSS 2. Evanston: Northwestern University Press.

2. Kuykendall, George Benson 1919. *History of the Kuykendall Family Since Its Settlement in Dutch New York.* Portland, OR: Kilham Stationery and Printing Co.. [From "Author's Reminiscences," no page numbers.]

3. From original notes by G.B. Kuykendall, in The Papers of George Benson Kuykendall, the Manuscripts, Archives and Special Collections, Holland Library, Washington State University.

4. Spier, Leslie and Edward Sapir 1930. *Wishram Ethnography,* UWPA 3 No. 3, p. 239. Seattle: University of Washington Press.

5. See "*Sam-a-lee-sack,*" p. 227, in Hines, Donald M. 1992. *Ghost Voices, Yakima Indian Myths, Legends, Humor and Hunting Stories.* Issaquah: Great Eagle Publishing, Inc..

6. "A Legend of *Enum-klah' pah,*" *Ghost Voices*:89-92.

7. Spier, *Wishram*:240.

8. Spier, *Wishram*:241.

9. Spier, *Wishram*:246.

PART TWO

CHAPTER ONE

AN EARLY INTRODUCTION TO THE SHAMAN AND FORMS OF MAGIC AMONG THE YAKIMA INDIANS

10. The text hereafter by George Benson Kuykendall, MD, was originally published as "The Indians of the Pacific Northwest—Their Mythical Creation, Gods of the *Wat-tee-tash* Age, Legends, Myths, Religion, Customs Relating to Marriage, Naming of Children, and Murder—Their Dances and Their Doctors—The Rehabiliment of the Dead, and Their Idea of a Future State," Chapter 60, in *History of the Pacific Northwest: Oregon and Washington.* . .[ed. Elwood Evans], Vol. II (Portland, OR: North Pacific History Company, 1889), see especially pp. 86-95. [Notes hereafter are by DH].

11. Found in The Papers of George Benson Kuykendall, in the Manuscripts, Archives and Special Collections, Holland Library, Washington State University, was a different or tentative draft of his publication on the shamans or power doctors, and the spirit beliefs of the Yakimas, "Indian Customs and Traditions." While the same essential order of topics occurs, and because many direct passages are found from the chapter cited above, I am persuaded that the particular or illustrative instances in this tentative draft were pruned from and should have appeared in Kuykendall's chapter in the *History of the Pacific Nortwest.* I have restored the illustrative material which *should have been originally included.* Of primary interest, this early document reflects Kuykendall's observations of life and lore among Central Washington Indian nations only seventeen years following the 1855 treaty at Walla Walla whereby great tracts of tribal lands were ceded away, and the reservation was created for the Yakimas and nearby tribes.

12. According to original notes by G.B. Kuykendall, the names of the tribes belonging to the Yakama [sic] Agency according to the treaty [of 1855] were as follows: "Yakima, Palouse, (Sa'ta's?), Pasquose, Nen'at-shapam, Klikitat, Kling-uit, Kow-was-saiy-se, Li-ay-was, Skinpah, Wish-am, Skyiks [Shyiks?], Ochecotes-Hamiltpa, Scaptcat—tribes in all."

13. George B. Kuykendall 1919. H*istory of the Kuykendall Family.* . .[no page numbers] previously cited.

14. Kuykendall, E[lgin] V. 1954. *Eighty Years in the Changing West.* Privately printed, p. 26.

15. E.V. Kuykendall:27.

16. E.V. Kuykendall:28.

17. For example, see the discussion of contagious / sympathetic magic in Frazer, J.G. 1961. *The New Golden Bough, A New Abridgment of the Classic Work*, ed. Theodor H. Gaster. New York: Doubleday & Co.,Inc., pp. 5-21.

18. Since the retelling of numerous Mid-Columbia traditional narratives on pp. 60-86 is not to our purpose here, especially as we have recently

published *Ghost Voices, Yakima Indian Myths, Legends, Humor and Hunting Stories*, Issaquah: Great Eagle Publishing, Inc., 1992 [435 pp.], we begin on pp. 86 ff. of Kuykendall's original text.

19. This is also spelled as *tahmahnawis* by McWhorter.

20. Kuykendall's notes on ordinary medicine vs. "spirit" medicine practices derive from his "Indian Customs and Traditions," undated typescript, pp. 5 ff., hereafter cited as "K".

21. See Spier, *Wishram*:236.

22. Murdock, Tenino:166.

23. Spier, *Wishram*:238.

24. Murdock, Tenino:168.

25. Spier, *Wishram*:238.

26. Murdock, Tenino:166. An age of six "or a little older" is cited.

27. Spier, *Wishram*:238.

28. Murdock, Tenino:166. Cited is the acquisition of "five spirits as lifetime helpers." Data by McWhorter and Spier do not support this detail.

29. Spier, *Wishram*:238.

30. Murdock, Tenino:166.

31. Murdock, Tenino:167. Cited here is that "shamanistic or curative" abilities came "after puberty."

32. Spier, *Wishram*:241. Although no Spirit Dance is mentioned by Kuykendall, still he cites the shaman's coming of age as an adult—when he realized his curative powers.

33. Spier, *Wishram*:236. Spier asserts there were *no* shamans' organizations among the Wishram. But see Murdock, Tenino:168. Murdock's sole informant, John Quinn, insisted ". . . the prospective shaman also had to pass the equivalent of a state medical board examination conducted by the shamans who had already been admitted to practice. These experienced practitioners led the neophyte to the edge of a high rim rock," where he was required to demonstrate his control over his spirits. Only Shamans, it was believed, could see and hear the guardian spirits of other people, and the theory was that they could judge the expertise of the neophyte in controlling his spirits on the test errands on which he was directed to dispatch them." The gist of the "examination" "seems clearly to have rested on

their collective estimate of his [neophyte's] personal characteristics, of his fitness to be entrusted with the exercise of great power" in order to be ". . . accepted by his seniors [shamans]."

34. Spier, *Wishram*:240.

35. Spier, *Wishram*:242. An instance of "self-cannibalism" is cited as occuring during the Spirit Dance. "Rows of scars" observed along some Indians' arms were also cited.

36. Spier, *Wishram*:238. But no training regiman is cited by Kuykendall.

37. Murdock, Tenino:166.

38. Murdock, Tenino:166-167.

39. Spier, *Wishram*:237f. recounts of very strong guardian spirits: the grizzly bear, sturgeon, or rattlesnake.

40. In his notes Kuykendall employs an alternate spelling: "*tlacha'cha* (spirit of the dead). If a youth's *tamanowash* power comes from the *Tlcha'cha* then he has "*Tlcha'cha tah.*"

41. Spier, *Wishram*:240.

42. Spier, *Wishram*:244.

43. Murdock, Tenino:170.

44. Spier, *Wishram*:247.

45. Spier, *Wishram*:246.

46. Murdock, Tenino:167.

47. See again Murdock, Tenino: 166.

48. Spier, *Wishram*:246.

49. Spier, *Wishram*:248.

50. Spier, *Wishram*:247. Spier notes that at death a patient was likely to name whomever had bewitched him/her.

51. Spier, *Wishram*:245.

52. Murdock, Tenino:168.

53. See again Spier, *Wishram*: 247.

54. Murdock, Tenino:170.

55. Spier, *Wishram*:246.

56. Spier, *Wishram*:244. Kuykendall's observations contest Spier's.

57. Spier, *Wishram*:245. Spier's term for the [major] shaman, male or female, doesn't coincide with that given by Kuykendall.

58. In his notes Kuykendall states: "the *pamiss pamiss itta*] are usually old women."

59. Kuykendall notes that "this appears to be two words so the above references to it should also be only two words, and not the last broken into "*pamiss itta*." Note the variant spelling in the previous note.

60. Spier, *Wishram*:255.

61. Spier, *Wishram*:245.

62. Spier, *Wishram*:245.

63. Spier, *Wishram*:242. Spier mentions, as an example, a "hat and belt of wolf skin" as emblematic of a *tah* spirit.

64. Murdock, Tenino:168.

65. Spier, *Wishram*:246. Kuykendall makes no mention of the shaman smoking before beginning the cure.

66. Spier, *Wishram*:246. Spier notes also of heating the hands at the fire and then placing them on the patient's belly.

67. Murdock, Tenino:167. But note the dual spirits which Murdock's sole informant insisted that each shaman had: a) for diagnosis; b) for therapy for soul loss, etc.

68. Murdock, Tenino:169. Cited by Kuykendall as part of the diagnostic process: sprinkling the patient with water. But Kuykendall makes no mention of: a) smoking; b) "blowing on a basket of water;" c) sending his diagnostic *tah* into a patient; d) immediately resigning the case if the offending spirit is too powerful for the shaman.

69. Spier, *Wishram*:236. Spier notes that the shaman was assisted by a speaker.

70. Murdock, Tenino:168.

71. Spier, *Wishram*:244.

72. Murdock, Tenino:169.

73. Murdock, Tenino:169.

74. Murdock, Tenino:169. No mention is made of the murder of the failed or inept shaman.

75. Cf. Matthew 8:30-32; Mark 5:11-13; Luke 8:32-33.

76. Kuykendall gives an alternate spelling: "*Skaie*."

77. Kuykendall notes: "I will describe it ["Dancing the Sticks"] as practiced formerly at the Cascades. The Indians say only a few can do such things among them." And Kuykendall's notes also mention the Wishrams as "stick-dancing."

78. Spier, *Wishram*:243-244. An episode of "dancing *tamanowash* sticks "of *Sa'lmin* (or *Wa'katca*?)" was told to Leslie Spier during 1924/25. Spier's account specifically identifies the sticks as percussion billets.

79. Spier, *Wishram*:270. Note that *five years* is cited by Spier.

80. Spier, *Wishram*:271.

81. Spier, *Wishram*:270.

82. Spier, *Wishram*:271.

83. Name of the deceased?

84. The particular range of mountains is unclear: Cascade Range? Bitteroots? Rockies?

85. This is likely Memmaloose Island in the Columbia River, a short distance downstream from The Dalles, Oregon.

86. But see narrative No. 38 "*Tahmahnawis* Power" in which use is made of a besom of rose branches to kill or drive away spirit traces of a dead woman.

87. Spier, *Wishram*:270.

88. Spier, *Wishram*:271. Kuykendall as well as McWhorter make this point. During the winter of 1885 when they resided among members of the Warm Springs Indian Reservation, Oregon, Jeremiah Curtin and his wife related of the Indians' "raising of the dead" when bodies of the deceased were taken up, wrapped in new blankets, and then buried anew.

CHAPTER TWO
THE ORIGINS OF SHAMANS' POWER OR *TAHMAHNAWIS*

89. See also Chapter Five hereafter in which the varied *tahmahnawis* powers of shamanic individuals are discussed (DH).

90. See "Winter Bathing," p. 191 in Sapir, Edward 1909. *Wishram Texts, Together with Wasco Tales and Myths*, II:PAES. Leyden: E.J. Brill. Sapir's informant McGuff confesses that he never acquired a spirit power.

91. See "The Dwarf Mountain People," pp. 67-68; cf. "The *Pah-ho-ho Klah*," pp. 15-17 in Hines, Donald M. 1991. *The Forgotten Tribes, Oral Tales of the Teninos and Adjacent MidColumbia River Indian Nations*. Issaquah: Great Eagle Publishing, Inc. And in *Ghost Voices...* see "The *Te-chum' Mah*," pp. 61-62; "The *Puh-tuh Num*," pp. 104-105; also "The *Schoptash*: 'Painted Rocks of the Naches,'" pp. 105-107 (DH).

92. Billie Stayhai, 1909.

93. Undoubtedly this is a reference to the spirit quest or vision quest which youths, both boys and girls, undertook at about age twelve.

94. In an undated note, McWhorter identifies several animals and the magic powers which might be obtained from them during a youth's spirit quest: "*Tahmahnawis* power derived from the grizzly bear imparts a fighting spirit, a proneness to bite and battle with everything with which its possessor comes in contact. The *tahmahnawis* derived from the wolf, also a fighter but more adroit than the grizzly (would similarly impart a fighting spirit). An Indian favored with the power of the wolf would excel in hunting. Tahmahnawis of the coyote [imparts] slyness and ability to slip upon, to skulk and to hide. *Tahmahnawis* of the jackrabbit [imparts] the endurance to run. *Tahmahnawis* of the fish or any aquatic animal [imparts] the ability to remain under water. *Tahmahnawis* of the rattlesnake [imparts] success in gambling."

95. Collected during December 1917. The narrative describes the visitation of a *tahmahnawis* spirit to a successful youth. But many shamans had more than one *tah* spirit (DH).

96. These are the Cascades or *Watlala* Indians whose original tribal area consisted of the banks of the Columbia River from below Hood River and now Bonneville Dam westward to approximately Sauvies Island and the mouth of the Willamette River at Portland, Oregon (DH).

97. See again note 88 above.

98. See again G.B. Kuykendall's observations, p. 43 above (DH).

99. The Chinook jargon was a trade language used at least by the tribes of Central Washington and Oregon (DH).

100. That is, the Yakima tongue.

101. Heard from *Laux-w'aptus* (One Feather), 1921.

102. Heard from Joe Tuckaho, Nez Perce, on July 5, 1922.

103. Note particularly that this informant made three unsuccessful attempts to obtain tahmahnawis power. Only on the fourth attempt did he apparently succeed (DH).

104. Heard from Tom Hill, warrior of the Nez Perce War of 1877, on July 5, 1911.

105. Heard from Simon Goudy, 1918.

106. Tribes close by the Yakimas relate of the *Te-chum' mah*, a mysterious elfin people. In *The Forgotten Tribes*. . ., see the Umatilla version: "The Dwarf Mountain People," pp. 61-62. In G*host Voices*. . ., see "The *Te-chum' mah*," pp. 61-62 (DH).

107. Heard from Mrs. Caesar Williams during January 1918.

108. I [L.V. McWhorter] know these two men who are still living. Black Wolf claims the chieftaincy of his band.

CHAPTER THREE
ACOUNTS OF SHAMANS DESCRIBE
THEIR HEALING POWERS WITH COR-
ROBORATIVE STATEMENTS BY THEIR PATIENTS

109. See "The *Tahmahnawis Bear*" in *Ghost Voices*:230 (DH).

110. Heard on the night of July 10, 1910, at the home of *Si-hol-tux*, better known as Charley *Schi-lo*, on the Yakima Indian Reservation, near White Swan, Washington. Informant was *Nah-Schoot*: ("sound," or "noise"), whose English name was Jacob Hunt, a Klickitat Medicine man and priest. William Charley was interpreter. I first met the"medicine man" at a council held at the home of Chief *Yoom-tee-bee* in June 1909. I then learned of his reputed power in curing members of his race of the drink habit. A medicine man and priest, *Nah-schoot* was a Klickitat, living at White Salmon, Washington. He died in 1915.

111. Unless the informant means that he saw his forebears in a vision, he learned tribal traditions and culture *from* his elders (DH).

112. *Nah-schoot* sees and hears in part a "death journey vision." See Chapter Six hereafter for eleven complete visions of a "death" journey (DH).

113. In former years, before the advent of the missionaries among the Klickitats and Yakimas, in short the entire Salishan family, worship was carried on in a kneeling posture, with aged men watching the votaries. Any show of levity, or disposition on the part of the young people to "court," was severely punished. The offender was summarily taken from the place of worship and whipped, with perhaps other penance inflicted. The worship dance was conducted on the knees.

114. *Nah-schoot* repeats of a prophetic vision (DH).

115. McWhorter notes that at this point *Nah-Schoot* inquired as to the belief of the white people regarding the destruction of towns and cities by fire and flood. [McWhorter] answered that some, like himself, believed that such disasters are Divine visitations for the wickedness of the people, while others regarded them as natural phenomena, resulting from certain temporal conditions. The narrator listened, then continued.

116. Again, for the Indian to speak of his *tah* power is to cause it to leave. This has happened to *Nah-schoot*. A similar sad occurrence is related to McWhorter by *Histo* in No. 31 "The Source of *Histo's* Power as a Warrior," hereafter (DH).

117. Given the following morning [July 11, 1910] after *Nah-Schoot's* narrative.

118. McWhorter asked: "What did you do with your jug of whiskey?" *Si-hol-tux* replied: "I broke that jug and never drank again." Testimony continued; William Charley was interpreter.

119. McWhorter notes that he was then circulating a petition on the Reservation asking for the annulling of all saloon licenses within the Yakima Country. The medicine man, *Nah-schoot* said: "This petition you have gotten up against the saloons. The Methodists want us to come to their church and sign this petition with them. We have no objection to their signing it; but if we had a [copy of the] petition to take to our meetings, we could sign it there. Of course we will work against liquor in every way. All of my people will sign this petition because we want to see this whiskey habit done away with. It is bad."

120. *Nah-schoot* here inquired what I [McWhorter] thought of his belief. I candidly replied that I considered it good, and that the Whites should recognize its merits and cease in their efforts at trying to break it down; that they would do well to pattern after some of its doctrines and efforts at bettering the condition of his people. *Nah-schoot* then continued: "This is what I learned, as the first Indians learned in early days. There came a man

who knew all things, how the world and all the people were created. How the foods and all things were made. Because of this, in the same way I came to learn all these things. I told my young people how we should live and be good. I thought to give you this, to tell you about it. You try, and . . . do make a help towards this belief. Report it, so it will be recognized by the Whites, as *our* belief. We should not oppose each other in works of good. We should all work together and not meddle with the belief of others."

121.   McWhorter notes that this man had received treatment the evening before. His ailment was drunkenness.

122.   While L.V. McWhorter is an observer-participant in this incident, his Indian informant is not identified (DH).

123.   These pictures and the little, ancient people who painted them are recounted in "The *Put-tuh num*," *Ghost Voices*:104-105 (DH).

124.   The identity of the woman and her husband is not given (DH).

125.   This is likely Chief George Waters (DH).

CHAPTER FOUR
THE RATTLESNAKE AS
SHAMAN'S SIMPLE

126.   See note 225 from "A Border Vision," hereafter.

127.   The likely informant is Louis Mann who elsewhere identifies his grandfather as *Wan'-tah*.

128.   *Wan'-tah* was supposed to have derived an occult power from the *wahk'-puch* [rattlesnake]. He sometimes killed the reptile and swallowed the two inner lobes of fat in the raw state. But *Wan'-tah* was not exclusive in this practice. At least one other medicine man of the Yakimas who survived *Wan'-tah* a few snows, was addicted to the same custom. Both acted in this respect, in compliance with the secret rules given them by their *tah*. It was "medicine," not food.

Wan'-tah was conversant with the formula for concocting the deadly poison from the poison-glands of the rattlesnake, and the rare species of spider found burrowing in the desert. [See No. 51 "How Grey Squirrel Drove the Buffalo," *Ghost Voices*:160-173. And see especially note 96 describing use of the poison of *Tesh-poon*, or the venomous trap-door spider.] He also knew the medicinal qualities of roots, herbs and insects. At one time he was dangerously ill for several days, his friends believing that he could not recover. One evening when at his worst, he called his little grandson and said: "My grandson! I am about to die. Go catch five *teech* and bring them to me alive. Get big ones. They will cure me." *Teech* is the large, black "stink-bug," so common in the desert regions.

In telling me of the incident long years afterwards, the grandson said: "I went out and soon had a big *teech*. I caught another one, then I caught two more. I caught another one, five in all. They were big ones, and they smelled badly." I took them to my grandfather who said: "They are what I want!" He pulled off their legs and ate them raw. The next morning my grandfather was well.

129. For mentions of the *Ke-nute'* in *Ghost Voices*. . . see "How the Mountain Broke," pp. 80-81; "Wisdom of the *Wah'k-puch*," pp. 82-83; and "The Story of the Lake at *Kh-nute*," pp. 94-95 (DH).

130. The fact that William Charley lived at White Swan, on the southerly edge of the Yakima Reservation, leads us to presume that he is the narrator of this segment (DH).

131. See again note 134 above.

132. Referred to here is the sickle blade of the mower, described from the vantage of the serpents, where both the material [steel] and the technology [a hay mower] were new and strange things (DH).

133. These are chokecherry bushes (DH).

134. This refers probably to the vicinity of modern Fort Simcoe, formerly the headquarters of the Indian Agency for the Yakima Reservation (DH).

135. The narrator is not identified.

136. Prophetic visions/dreams while asleep or even awake are common to the Shaman. See again "The *Tahmahnawis* Bear," *Ghost Voices*:230 where the medicine man *Chow-yayh-les* warns *Sam-a-lee-sack* from hunting bear as a result of having dreamt an ominous dream of a bloody bear with a bad *tah* spirit (DH).

137. This and following narratives were given to L.V. McWhorter during 1909 by Chief *We-yal-lup Wa-ya-cika*. Like *Wan'-tah*, *We-yal-lup Wa-ya-cika* obtained his *tahmahnawis* power from the rattlesnake. McWhorter notes that the chief's occult name was given him by the *Wah'k-puch* [rattlesnake]: *Let-h*: "Shining" or "bright," like the sun's rays reflected on crusted or frozen snow. The Yakima guttural sound to the name is not given in McWhorter's notes. Indeed, *Yal-lup* was thought or supposed to possess a "power" conferred on him by the *Wah'k-puch*. In councils when sitting cross-legged, often his foot was seen to quiver with a peculiar rapid motion, supposedly the vibration of that serpent's rattles. The narratives hereafter relate of the dimensions of his magic, his healing powers deriving from his *tah*, the spirit of the *wah'k-puch*.

138. *Mo-loc*: name of a noted rattlesnake den on the south slope of Ahtanum Mountain, on the *"Yallup"* Road." It must be four miles from the Goudy ranch. Rattlers in vast numbers hibernate there. The entrance is a small hole under a shelf of the cliff, where the odor is very nauseating even in the coldest of weather. To put your head in this *Wah'k-puch* house is a temerity to be punished by swift and severe illness of which the writer [L.V. McWhorter] can well attest from personal experience.

139. *Pah-to-sah* ("Animal lying down.") This name is applied to an oblong hillock standing on the desert plain, on the Simon Goudy allotment about two-and-a-half miles east of White Swan, Washington, Yakima Indian Reservation. Lying within the interior of the mound is, supposedly, an animal not unlike an elk. Nothing is known further of the legend.

140. Numerous accounts relate of mammoth rattlesnakes, some with horns, etc. In *Ghost Voices* see "Why the Rattlesnake Crawls," pp. 48-49; "How the Mountain Broke," pp. 80-81; "Wisdom of the *Wah'k-puch*," pp. 82-83; and *"Tho'-wit-tet*," pp. 103-104 (DH)

141. The chief's direct approach for money from McWhorter is interesting indeed. I can recall no previous bid for "Cash for Lore" of McWhorter (DH).

142. This story of the Zillah Monster was apparently lost with the death of Chief *We-yal-lup Wa-ya-cika* December 17, 1915. It is possible among the older Yakimas the legend may still linger, but I have found none who could tell me anything about it. Bones of some prehistoric animal, presumably the mastadon have been unearthed in a brickyard at Granger, on the Yakima [River], only a few miles west of Zillah, [Washington].

143. Heard in 1910.

144. The medicine man was boastfully proclaiming his ability to retrieve and restore the youth's *spirit*, or *life*, even though apparent death had claimed the stricken child. A comatose state was also referred to as death by the Indians. See especially Chapter Six hereafter (DH).

145. Charles Mann was a prominent tribesman of his day, the father of Louis Mann of later notoriety. He died January 9, 1901.

146. "Brother-in-law;" "sister-in-law;" "uncle;" "aunt;" "nephew;" "niece;" "cousin;" "grandfather" and "grandmother" are terms ofttimes, as in the foregoing case, used solely to denote deep esteem and respect, an abiding faith in the integrity of the one addressed. In one instance coming under my personal observation, a prominent tribesman in writing to the Head Chief addressed him: "My Dear Nephew," and subscribed himself: "Your Nephew."

147. McWhorter notes that Chief We-*yal-lup Wa-ya-cika*, an outstanding medicine man of the Yakimas, noted for his hidden, occult forces, gave him this information when commenting on the subject of the mist brought up by the Nez Perce invocator smoking. (The context for the Chief's remarks is unknown).

"Yes, it is true," he said. "I knew some people here who could do those things. They are now all gone. Young children going to school do not learn this wisdom.

"One man would say,'It will rain tomorrow,' or, 'It will rain tomorrow night.' When the time came, that man would call his power, and if no rain and wind, that man would die. These things are true. Yellow Wolf did not lie." [See McWhorter, L.V. 1940. *Yellow Wolf: His Own Story*. Caldwell, ID: The Caxton Printers, Ltd.]

It is related of *We-yallup* that he was summoned to treat an Indian lad at the Agency school who had been bitten by a rattlesnake, and [was] given up by the Agency physician to die. After examining the little sufferer, the medicine man went out into the open and, seating himself on an isolated boulder where there was solitude, filled his pipe and proceeded to smoke. It was not long until dark clouds began overspreading a hitherto clear sky, and there fell a shower of rain and hail. From that hour, a change for the better was discernable in the patient, who was soon restored to complete health. It would be difficult to convince the older tribesmen against the potency of the *prayer-smoke*.

148. McWhorter notes of a series of questions he posed, and answers from *We-yal-lup Wa-ya-cika*:
McW: Would you have killed the *wah'k-puch* had it not bitten you?

We: No! Only hit him easy. Make him stay away from trail. I will tell you this. I think you are a good man, my friend. I have not told these stories to anybody. In Washington, D.C., a man wanted me to tell them to him. He looks poor, does not look good and fine. He is from across the water. [The Indians' picture of an anthropologist? An Indian's response to Boas, or Sapir?]. I did not tell him. I see that you have a good blanket on your saddle. Maybe you give me that blanket? [A second instance of *We-yal-lup Wa-ya-cika* boldly seeking "pay for lore."]

McW: To this direct flattery and test of friendship, I replied: "That is an old blanket. Like the saddle offered you for saving *Wee-ah-nee-tla* [see "Boy Bitten by a *Wah'k-puch*" above], it is second-hand. I would be ashamed to give you such a blanket. You would be ashamed to let your friends see it. You know all about the *wah'k-puch*. You have seen the *head chief* of the *Wah'k-puch*. You have great power from him. You are growing old. Tell me the story of this horned chief, that I may write it down and not let it die with you. I will then give you a blanket of which you will be proud, and I will not be ashamed of before the people."

We: This seemed to please the aged Chief, and he spoke: "Your words sound good. Not now, but some day when we have more time I will tell you all. [The medicine man's manifest reluctance to speak of the great horned Chief of the *wah' k-puch* is accounted for in the fact that he obtained his *tah*, or power from this scarce seen and fancied reptile. It was in the *Titon* [Tieton] [where he met the monster, where he communed with it whenever he went to the canyon. . . .. Ofttimes when assembled in council, and the old chief became animated or unduly aroused, his foot would be observed to vibrate not unlike the tail of the rattler when disturbed. This was an unconscious manifestation of the *power* conferred upon him by the *wah'k-puch* Chief.]

"Now I am telling you this. My father, like me had power from the *wah'k-puch*. Some can take them in their bosoms. I do not do this. [But see episode above where the chief carries a live rattler about in his pocket]. But if you do not believe me; [do not] believe what I am tell you, I will handle one for you. No! I do not pull their fangs. I take him without hurting him and play tricks with him. The *wah'k-puch* knows me.

"In Washington, D.C., I wanted to make a show. Captain Eanius was with me. We were broke. I will play with *wah'k-puch* and get money. We must find *wah'k-puch*. "A crowd said to us: 'Go to the park and see animals.' "We go there. We see lots of animnals: lizards, reptiles. We find snakes. I size them up. Big ones! Some thicker than big tepee pole. Head broader than berry basket.

"I think: 'I never see so big snakes anywhere. I will get him and show tricks with him.' Then I get afraid! I do not know this *puch* [snake]. If he was Yakima *wah'k-puch*, I would not be afraid of him."

149.   It would appear from this declaration that the Chief was, at the time, *Walleme*; "secret medicine man," who had not yet publicly proclaimed his profession. *Twa'-tee* is a "public" or "open" medicine man. None ever attempt to practice their powers before attaining middle age.

150.   Narrator not identified.

151.   This narrative was written down at Ahtanum Res., Washington, Dec. 24th, 1915, by Louis Charles Mann, a Yakima bad brave, so-called by a white man in this country. Mann appends a final, difficult-to-read note: "McWhorter here is for your story book no for news paper regulate it good I was in town but in a hurry christmas morning Louis Mann" [sic] (DH).

152.   Louis Mann's original version has been considerably edited; spelling, paragraphs, sentences, verbs, and punctuation have been regularized to improve ease of reading. The subject content of the piece has had nothing added, nothing deleted (DH).

153. This is an interesting version of the story of Noah and the flood. See Genesis 6-8. But see also motif A1018 Flood as punishment (DH).

CHAPTER FIVE
REMARKABLE ACCOUNTS OF
SHAMANS' *TAHMAHNAWIS* POWERS

154. For one version of a narrative about *Nash-lah*, a destructive water-being who lived at the great falls [Celilo], formerly near present-day The Dalles, Oregon, see "*Nash-lah,*" *The Forgotten Tribes*:12-15.

155. Heard from Louis Mann.

156. Heard from Medicine Owl, 1911.

157. *An-a-whoa* (Black Bear) narrated to McWhorter two tales: "The Bridge of the Gods;" also "*Nash-lah,*" in *The Forgotten Tribes*:12-15. Her father was captured by *Cili-cola*, the daughter of *Nash-lah*. They were married, and he lived many snows with his river-wife, sometimes coming ashore to see his own people. Finally, he disappeared never to be seen again. When the canoes of the Indians were threatened by the boiling, downward suction of the water so common on the *n-Che'-wana*, the occupant had but to call: "We are relations of *Cili-cola*," when the danger would instantly subside.

   The marriage of a youth to the daughter of a river spirit is a major element in "The Disobedient Boy," pp. 100-103 in Hines, Donald M. 1984. *Tales of the Nez Perce*. Fairfield, WA: Ye Galleon Press. The tale is related elsewhere over the Southern Plateau Area (DH).

158. Heard from Mrs. George Waters during November 1918.

159. Located about 45 miles east of Issaquah along Interstate 90, Lake Kachess is the focus of a number of Yakima legends which describe its mysterious quality (DH).

160. Included here are accounts of how *tahmahnawis* powers were obtained by warriors, etc. See also Chapter One and accounts of particular *tah* powers obtained by Yakima shamans (DH).

161. Heard from William Charley during September 1911.

162. *Histo* (also known as *Schablo*), was half Deschutes (Tenino?) and half Wasco. He belonged to the Deschutes Indians, who dwelt in the vicinity of the mouth of the Tenino [sic] River at the Columbia River.

163. Heard from *Histo* on 3 Sept. 1916. William Charley was interpreter.

164. See No. 32 "*Histo's* Narrative of his Father" hereafter (DH).

165. By telling McWhorter details of the origin and employment of his *tah* power, *Histo* has caused the *tah* to leave him (DH).

166. See again note 164 above.

167. Wasco Jim served as interpreter for *Histo*.

168. A vivid example of homoeopathic magic in which the young life [spirit] is taken in by the ill or dying man, that he might recover (DH).

169. The hawk wings referred to, *Histo* gave me before I left the Indian camp. They were long feathers of both right and left wings, well preserved, with ends of the feathers clipped off. The *right* wing contains five feathers, with an ornamentation of one red, and some three or four small green feathers fastened at the base. The fiber has been stripped from the base of the main feathers two to four inches.

   The *left* wing contains eight feathers, and its base is strengthened with a small wrapping of pink stripped calico, and ornamented with a bit of white weasel, or ermine skin and three small green feathers. These wings were worn by *Histo* during both the Modoc and Bannock wars. They were tied to his hair at the back of his head, below the crown, and were regarded as a charm from the bullets of the enemy.

170. Date and informant not given.

171. Heard in a hunting camp during April 1923.

172. Date and informant not given.

173. Date and informant not given.

174. See "Bear Woman of the Nespelems," *Ghost Voices*:178-180; also "Indian Aversion to Killing Bear," pp. 266-268 (DH).

175. Heard during 1918.

176. See again note 88 above.

177. Likely, this is Memaloose Island, just downriver from The Dalles, Oregon. See note 85 above.

178. Told by *I-keep-swah* (Sitting Rock), July 1918. Sitting Rock's Christian name was Jim Peter; he was also known as "Wasco Jim."

179. The "Mount Hood People" are recounted in manuscript: "*Ah-ton-o kah* of *She-ko-un*," a legend of five dwarfs inhabiting Mount Hood (DH).

180. Date or informant not given.

181. As McWhorter notes, the number **5** occurs repeatedly and traditionally throughout the folk narratives of the Yakimas and neighboring tribes. See especially folk narrative motifs: Z71.3. Formulistic number: five; also D1273.1.2.1. Magic numbers: **five** (DH).

182. Heard in an Indian hunter camp during April 1921.

183. Date and informant not given.

184. Heard during April 1927.

185. Such drumming employed during a shamanic "performance" is cited by Spier, *Wishram*:243,246 (DH).

186. Use of a "spokesman" during a shamanic "performance" is cited by Spier, *Wishram*:246 (DH).

187. Date and informant not given.

188. Date and informant not given.

189. Heard in an Indian hunters camp during April 1921. This narrative also appears in *The Forgotten Tribes*:65 (DH).

190. Date and informant not given.

CHAPTER SIX
SOME MID-COLUMBIA TRIBAL TALES
RECOUNTING THE
DEATH JOURNEY VISION

191. This chapter appeared previously in *Northwest Anthropological Research Notes* 25 (1991):31-56. We are grateful to Prof. Roderick Sprague for permission to reprint.

192. This excerpt derives from a transcription of an undated manuscript prepared by Carol Thompson, et al., in 1973: "Indian Traditions, Legends, Superstitions, and Customs," in The Papers of George Benson Kuykendall, Washington State University Libraries, Pullman, Washington. See Hines, Donald M. 1976. *An index of Archived Resources for a Folklife and Cultural History of the Inland Pacific Northwest Frontier*. Ann Arbor, University Microfilms International, p. 51. Kuykendall's original sentencing and spelling have been retained. Where needed, punctuation has been inserted for clarity. (All notes hereafter—DH).

193. Studies of "after death experiences," or visions of the "life beyond," are very numerous indeed. Listed here are but a few of the most useful works which include extensive bibliographies for the inquiring student.

    Kubler-Ross, Elizabeth 1974. *On Death and Dying*. New York: Macmillan; Moody, Raymond A. 1976. *Life After Life*. New York: Bantam Books; Rawlings, Maurice S. 1978. *Beyond Death's Door*. New York: Bantam Books.

194. See Nelson A. Ault, comp. 1959. *The Papers of Lucullus Virgil McWhorter*. Pullman: Friends of the [W.S.U.] Library.

195. See "Vision of Charley," and "Vision of Dick Benson," in Spier, *Wishram*: 252-253.

196. According to Howell, Erle 1965. *Methodism in the Northwest*, ed. by Chapin D. Foster. Nashville: Parthenon Press, Father J. [James] H. [Harvey] Wilbur is described as "high-minded," "efficient," even "forceful" when required. Elsewhere, he is also described as intolerant, arrogant regarding the Indians. If the fearsome substance, the style of Wilbur's pulpit manner are difficult to come by, some measure of him might have been seen in his proteges, including the Rev. George Waters, brother of Yakima Chief White Swan [Joe Stwire]. Howell notes, "George Waters had held a revival among the Nez Perces at Lapwai [Idaho] with 146 converts."

197. According to Sapir in 1905, "of the three Christian sects now represented among the Indians of the Yakima Reservation (Catholics, Methodists, and Shakers), the Shakers are probably the most religious. A number of Wishram hymns and religious texts are in use among them," Sapir, Wis*hram*:191-192.

198. Spier, *Wishram*:133 notes that "there were no ceremonials not connected with shamanistic rites."

199. In a miscellaneous note, based on "Information obtained April 1927," McWhorter states: "There are, at this time at least fourteen or sixteen 'medicine' men and women on the Yakima Indian Reservation." His informant may have been Sam *Poyat*, noted then among the Yakimas as a very strong shaman.

200. According to Spier, *Wishram*:236, "The spirits from which power was obtained were animals, birds, reptiles, insects, and fish, that is, inhabitants of the physical world, not the physical world itself. Their number was large; there were mentioned: grizzly and common bear, buffalo, wolf, coyote, cougar, wild cat, deer, mountain animals generally; eagle, raven, birds of the mountains, lakes and rivers generally, both large and small; rattlesnake, mountain lizard, turtle; sturgeon; insects; thunder. The list is not complete."

201. See McGuff's recounting of the harsh midwinter bathing in ice-covered waters which he experienced for falling asleep while listening to the old men telling "myths" —Sapir *Wishram*:189-191.

202. See "The Shaman's Inaugural Dance," in Spier *Wishram*: 240-241. And see also "Shamans' Performances," p. 241, concerning the spirit dances held mainly in midwinter: "Each person, men and women sang but once during the night, but they might repeat the song for as many nights as the affair continued. They never sang in this fashion by day."

203. Spier, *Wishram*:241 recounts that during the dancing the successful quester's family gave away gifts.

204. See Spier *Wishram*:239-240.

205. In Sapir *Wishram*: 191 McGuff recounts: "But not at all have I seen anything that they call a guardian spirit. I do not know what it is like. Sometimes, although there is no ice in the river, it is present in a canoe or a boat; in that same water I would bathe myself. In winter the water of a boat or canoe always freezes, which is just a little bit cool."

206. Very insightful is Noll, Richard 1985. "Mental Imagery Cultivation as a Cultural Phenomenon: The Role of Visions in Shamanism," *Current Anthropology* 26:443-461. See especially p. 449: "The nascent shaman may be characterized by what has been called the 'fantasy-prone personality.' And Wilson and Barber (1981, 1982) compiled a profile from an intensive study of excellent hypnotic subjects and concluded that "fantasy-prone personalities' may comprise 4% of the population."

207. The narrator of No. 1 "Dream Presentiment of Death" is *An-a-whoa* (Black Bear). Traditional tales among the Yakima and Wishram/Wasco recount of the 'Orpheus tale,' of Coyote's journey to the land of the dead in an attempt to bring back to everlasting life his daughter, wife, etc. Not only is the explanation for the eternal presence of death in man's life of interest, but also the peripheral details of the place of death (where the dead dwell). See esp. No. 56 "Coyote Goes to the Land of the Dead," *Ghost Voices*:190-191. Klickitat, Wasco, Wishram and other Plateau Indian peoples recount this tale too.

208. In note 37 to "*Tah-tah Kle-Ah*," *Ghost Voices*:63-65, McWhorter describes not only the Yakimas' fear of the rattlesnake, which abounds in sectors of the reservation, but also their revulsion at possibly eating the serpent.

209. See Spier *Wishram*:270.

210. See "Acquiring Power" in Spier, *Wishram*:238-240. See also "The Shaman's Inaugural Dance," pp. 240-241; also "Shaman's Performance," pp. 241-244.

211. While the death journey vision narratives seem in substance to constitute new oral forms within Yakima-Wishram culture, yet in fact the new ideas conform with old structures thanks to the tenacity of oral tradition. In order to further prove out the traditionality of these narratives, I have held them up against Okrik's Laws—a very high degree of correlation is evident. See Olrik, Axel 1965. "Epic Laws of Folk Narratives." Alan Dundes, ed. *The Study of Folklore*. Englewood Cliffs, N.J., Prentice-Hall, Inc., pp. 129-141. And the scope of Olrik's Epic Laws in American Indian materials has previously been investigated by Lund, Astrid 1908. "Indiansk sagn digtning og de episke lawe," *Danske Studier*, 5:175-188

In order to further prove out the traditionality of these narratives, they have been held up against Olrik's Laws. A very high degree of correlation is evident.

   A. As Olrik observed, these tales open not abruptly but gradually, invariably with a description (either by McWhorter or from the informant) of an illness or great personal injury [the initial frame] by which the informant is rendered gravely afflicted and, as a result, "dies." Accounts 50, 56, 57, 58, 59, and 60 open with an account of a grave illness; accounts 52 and 53 begin with an account of some bloody accident. But narratives 51, 54 and 55 open with no malady, or none clearly stated. Concomitantly, upon the protagonist's relating the vision proper, after "waking from death," the vision does not end abruptly but continues with a statement of activity upon return to life, of gradual terminal calm—[the closing of the frame.] Still more, the death journey vision serves at least two purposes: signify the need for penance; likely signify the imminence of the final death of the central figure. The final statement (frame) as supplied by the informant and even by McWhorter, underscores specifically that the death omen serves a warning to prepare for death (one's own or others): (50, 52, 53, 54, 55, 56, 57, 58, 59, 60). But no such precept or omen is evident in no. 51. The death journey vision does require the revived person to do penance, to confess wrongs (53, 55, 56, 58, 60) and to rid self of stolen objects no. 56. Further, the death journey vision calls for those revived to live right, to preach to others (52, 54, 55, 57, 59, 60). Finally, no purpose is present or clear in no. 50 or 54 (in which there are no whites in the "good world)." And backsliding is revealed of the revived protagonist in no. 52.

   B. The Law of Repetition (employment of repetition to gain emphasis) appears. Multiples of scenes occur in no. 52—6 scenes which reflect of four wrongs; no. 53—three segments of the vision: going up, explicitly going back; no. 54—three scenes of three occurences— going up, traversing, returning back home or nine repetitions [3 x 3 = 9]; no.59—five scenes visited/viewed occur. Multiples occur of described items in no.50—mounted band circles house three times; action repeated three times; no. 55— three sins; no. 56—two stolen items; no. 57—four men + one Indian; drink teas for five days; no. 60—two wrongs. But note in nos. 51, 53 and 58 no multiples appear as these texts are essentially monoepisodic.

C. While Emphasis comes Through Repetition, the particular number is important: often" 3", more likely " 5." Three repetitions occur in no. 50 (riders circle house three times)(details are repeated three times); no. 53 (three vision segments); no. 54 (three scenes are repeated three times); No. 55 (three sins); no. 56 (a wait of three days); no. 59 (revival comes on third day)(corpse to be buried on third day); no. 60 (person lives three days)(occurences repeated three times). Four repetitions: None. Five repetitions occur in no. 58 (five men drink teas five days); no. 59 (five items are mentioned). Other numbers include two: no. 56 (two stolen items). None; no number mentioned: nos. 51 and 58.

D. According to Olrik's Law of Two to a Scene, only two characters should appear and interact in any scene of a narrative. This can be seen in no. 50 (protagonist and a group); no. 51 (protagonist and children or a voice:); no. 52 (protagonist and a voice); no. 53 (protagonist and "someone"); no. 54 (protagonist and "a person"); nos. 55 and 56 (protagonist and "voice"); no.60 (protagonist and "Great Man"). Mixed numbers of characters occur in no. 52 (in scene B, for example, the protagonist + voice + a minor character, the woman); no. 59 (major scenes and minor scenes are overheard, are seen at a distance). Numeration absent: no. 58.

E. According to Olrik's Law of Contrast, the major characters appearing in each scene are strongly polarized, are opposites. Most often: we see (mortal "crossing over" vs. "A man" [God himself?"]:" (51, 52, 53, 55, 56, 58, 60). Exceptions occur when the Protagonist and a group are seen, or no contrast is apparent: (50, 54, 57 and 59).

F. Olrik's Law of Twins is not apparent due to the brevity and the nature of these narratives.

G. According to Olrik the Importance of *Initial* and *Final Positions* is reflected in that the principal character enters first: coming last is the person for whom our sympathy is aroused. But in the death journey visions positioning is not clear. First, the texts are quite simple in form, even monoepisodic in structure. Second, a series of persons or of events is often absent. Third, the protagonist remains important, a subject of sympathy from first to last: he/she is a) confronted with the need to reform; b) directed to preach that others reform; c) directed to publicly confess, lay bare his/her sinful nature.

H. Olrik's eighth law, Description Through Action, is certainly apparent in narratives, nos. 50, 52, 53, 54, 55, 56, 57, 59, and 60. Due to their brevity nos. 51 and 58 are not conclusive.

I. Olrik's ninth law calls for a Single-Stranded Plot, with no minor plot sequences, which is certainly apparent in nos. 50, 51, 53, 54, 55, 56, 58 (but see extended, appended portion); also 60. Such conciseness of plot is not conclusively found in nos. 52, 57, 59 (see major scenes / minor scenes).

J. Olrik's Law of the appearance of only salient and striking, necessary details, or Patterning, is present in nos. 50, 52, 53, 54, 56, 57, 58, 59 and 60. Patterning is not conclusively present in nos. 51 or 55.

K. Olrik's law of Tableau Scenes which "etch themselves in one's memory," is widely apparent in the death journey visions. Such scenes appear in no. 50 (circling procession of the dead); no. 52 (confrontation with the persona of his sins)(the figure of the King of the Underworld); no. 53 (scenes of earth's destruction); no. 54 (scenes of plenty)(scenes of beloved people who remain silent); no. 56 (casting off of stolen goods—done outside the dream vision itself); no. 57 (barred from the good place by a blood-stained man); no. 58 (threat of being served cooked rattlesnake to eat); no. 59 (vision of the damned-the several doomed chiefs (pattern of the good life)(confrontation with one's own flaws)(picture of the good land); no. 60 (death omen given to three men listening)(confession of brutality against wife)(confession of unfaithfulness to wife). Still, in some narratives here tableau scenes are not conclusively to be found, or the narrative is too limited in scope: nos. 51 and 55.

L. The Law of Logic of the Sage by which plausibility is based not on external reality, but on internal validity [including animism, esp. miracle and magic] appears in 50, 52, 53, 54, 57, 58, 59, 60, but is not conclusive for nos. 51, 55, 56, 58.

M. Olrik's Law of Unity of Plot prevails in that each narrative element works within the narrative to create an event, the possibility of which the reader had seen right from the beginning. In the death vision narratives the sense of each narrative possessing a distinct beginning, middle, and end includes nos. 50, 52, 53, 54, 56, 57 and 59 and 60 (poorly). Narratives in which unity of plot is much less evident, or not conclusive include 51, 55 and 58.

N. Olrik's Law of Concentration on One Leading Character is certainly evident in the narratives. The death journey visions display single stranded plots in which the emphasis rests upon the leading character's account of personal, extralife experiences. The protagonist (the person recounting the narrative) appears in nos. 50, 52, 53, 56, 58, 59 and 60. However, some narratives show variances or are inconclusive: 51, 54, 55 (the protagonist—person/other personnae are cited); no. 58 (protagonist—third person—god? plus a long epilogue: [third Indian person].

212. In traditional tales from over the Plateau Region, the number 5 is favored,

also **3**.

213. See McWhorter manuscript, "Bridge of the Gods."

214. Heard perhaps a short time after *An-a-whoa's* death. McWhorter's informant is Mrs. Caesar Williams (*Yes-to-lah-lemy*) with her husband (*Lo-pah-kin*).

215. But see mention below of *An-a-whoa's* near blindness.

216. Date and informant are unknown. McWhorter notes that to the Indian, an unconscious or comatose state is "being dead." "My wife died twice in one night but came back to life again," wrote a Warm Springs man in telling of an epidemic in his household.

217. Collected during autumn 1921, the informant not given.

218. According to McWhorter, the belief of these Indians is that intimacy with other than a woman of their own race debars them from the Happy Hunting Grounds forever.

219. Collected by L.V. McWhorter from *I-keeps-swah* (Sitting Rock), also known as James Peter or Wasco Jim, during c. 1925. McWhorter also notes: "*I-keep-swah* was born at *Win-quat*, "moving sands" or "washing sands," the Wasco name for what is now The Dalles, Oregon, about 1828. His father was half Klickitat and half Wasco. His mother, *Goos-hpah*, was half Wasco and half *Wishom* Wishram). Both these tribes were warlike, speaking much the same language. *I-keep-swah* was baptized in youth by the Roman Catholics and christened "Jim Peter." "Peter" was the Christian name of his father. Both were warriors in their day. *I-keep-swah* is also known as *Wasco Jim*. Of this name, when questioned, he said, "That is only fun-making name, whiskey name. Used to I drink lots of whiskey. Injuns give me that name, shame name."

220. Collected by Leslie Spier from an informant called "Charley," c. 1924-25. This vision appears in Spier, *Wishram*:252-253.

221. Collected by Leslie Spier from Mrs. Mabel Teio, c. 1924-25. This vision appeared originally in Spier *Wishram*:253.

222. Collected during March 1925, the informant not identified. The text was handwritten, perhaps hurriedly, on two pages.

223. Collected by L.V. McWhorter, time and informant unknown. Since McWhorter's Yakima acquaintance, Louis Mann, often refers to himself in his letters as a "bad Indian," etc., we presume that he was the informant.

224. Time and informant not identified.

225. The Yakimas' fear of the rattlesnake, which abounds in sectors of the reservation, but also their revulsion at possibly eating the serpent are recounted in note 37 of *"Tah-tah Kle'ah," Ghost Voices*:328.

226. Collected from *Sin-i-tah*, date unknown.

227. Informant and date not given. But if *An-a-whoa* is the spouse of *Ta'-chens*, then we presume that the informant was their daughter, *Yes-to-lah-lemy* (Mrs. Caesar Williams).

228. McWhorter notes: A true interpretation of these lines reflects no discredit on the character of Indian mothers. A contrast between the lives of the adult and that of small children was sharply intended. As compared with the moral lives of the men, a hidden compliment is accorded the woman; since their walks alone could be thought of as most nearly approaching that of the innocent child. The primitive-minded Yakima believes that the small child is sinless, and that nothing can stand between it and a happy existence in the hereafter. The highest type of adult life, as found in motherhood, was used in this almost scriptural illustration of the constituent elements entering into a strictly pure and faultless existence.

229. Interesting to note that *Ta-chens* relates with remorse of his beatings of his wife, *An-a-whoa*. Not only do we get a brief glimpse of marital stress and strife among Indian marrieds, we see more. *An-a-whoa*, like her husband, was party to revelations, as listed in "Dream Presentiment of Death," above. We would presume that similar personality profiles were present in the couple. But particularly of interest, the revelations to which they were party [our data here is most scant] were apparently dissimilar in substance: the wife's vision above recalls a most traditional Indian death-departure; the husband's vision recalls perhaps a Shakeristic death and hereafter: of a heaven-like place, or of a hell-like place.

SELECTED LIST OF READINGS

Ault, Nelson A 1959. *The Papers of Lucullus Virgil McWhorter.* Pullman, WA: Friends of the Library.

Barbeau, Marius 1958. *Medicine-Men on the North Pacific Coast,* NMCB 152, Anthro. Series 42. Ottawa: Department of Northern Affairs and National Resources.

Barnett, Homer G. 1957. *Indian Shakers, A Messianic Cult of the Pacific Northwest.* Champagne: Southern Illinois University Press

Bean, Lowell J. 1976. "California Indian Shamanism and Folk Curing," in *American Folk Medicine: A Symposium,* ed. Wayland D. Hand, pp. 109-123. Berkeley: University of California Press.

Benedict, Ruth F. 1923. *The Concept of the Guardian Spirit in North America.* American Anthroopological Association, Memoirs 29.

Boas, Franz 1893. "Doctrine of Souls and Disease Among the Chinook Indians," *Journal of American Folklore* 6:39-43.

Bourke, John G. 1892. *The Medicine-Men of the Apache,* 9th Annual Report, BAE, 1887-1888, pp. 451-596. Washington, D.C.: US Government Printing Office.

Chamberlain, Alexander F. 1901. "Kootenay Medicine Man," *Journal of American Folklore* 14:95-99.

Corlett, William T. 1935. *The Medicine Man of the American Indian And His Cultural Background.* Springfield, Ill.: Charles C. Thomas.

Dixon, Roland B. 1904. "Shamans of Northern California," *Journal of American Folklore* 17:23-27.

———— 1908. "Some Aspects of the American Shaman," *Journal of American Folklore* 21:1-12.

Dow, James 1986. *The Shaman's Touch: Otomi Indian Symbolic Healing.* Salt Lake City: University of Utah Press. Biblio., pp. 159-173.

DuBois, Cora 1938. *The Feather Cult of the Middle Columbia,* General Series in Anthropology 7. Menasha, Wi: George Banta.

Elmendorf, William W. 1989. *Northwest Coast: Skokomish [Shamanism]*,in *Witchcraft and Sorcery of the American Native Peoples*, ed. Deward E. Walker, Jr., pp. 75-111. Moscow: University of Idaho Press.

Gaster, Theodor H. ed. 1961. *The New Golden Bough, A New Abridgement of the Classical Work*, by Sir J. G. Frazer. See "The Roots of Magic," pp. 5-21. Garden City, N.Y.: Doubleday and Co., Inc.

Gatschet, A.S. 1893. "Medicine Arrows of the Oregon Indians," *Journal of American Folklore*, 6:111-112.

Grim, John 1983. *The Shaman: Patterns of Religious Healing Among the Ojibway Indians*. Norman: University of Oklahoma Press.

Haeberlin, H.K. 1907. *"Sbeted'aq*, A Shamanistic Performance of the Coast Salish," *American Anthropologist* 20:249-257.

Hines, Donald M. 1991. *The Forgotten Tribes, Oral Tales of the Teninos and Adjacent Mid-Columbia River Indian Nations*. Issaquah, WA: Great Eagle Publishing, Inc..

_____ 1976. *An Index of Archived Resources for a Folklife and Cultural History of the Inland Pacific Northwest Frontier*. Ann Arbor: University Microfilms International.

_____ 1992. *Ghost Voices, Yakima Indian Myths, Legends, Humor and Hunting Tales*. Issaquah, WA: Great Eagle Publishing, Inc..

_____ 1984. *Tales of the Nez Perce*. Fairfield, WA: Ye Galleon Press.

Hultkrantz, Åke 1953. *Conceptions of the Soul, Among North American Indians, A Study in Religious Ethnology*, Monograph Series I. Stockholm: The Ethnographical Museum of Sweden.

_____ 1992. *Shamanic Healing & Ritual Drama: Health & Medicine in Native American Religious Traditions*. New York: Crossroad Publications.

Hunn, Eugene S. 1990. *Nch'i-Wan'a, "The Big River:" Mid-Columbia Indians and Their Land*. Seattle: University of Washington Press. Biblio. pp. 295-309.

Jelik, Wolfgang 1982. *Indian Healing, Shamanic ceremonialist in the Pacific Northwest Today*. Blaine, Wa.: Hancock House Publishers.

Kelly, Isabel T. 1936. "Chemehuevi Shamanism," in *Essays in Honor of Alfred L. Kroeber*, pp. 129-142. Berkeley: University of California Press.

_____ 1939. "Southern Paiute Shamanism," *Anthropological Records* [Berkeley] 2:151-167.

Kubler-Ross, Elizabeth 1974. *On Death and Dying.* New York: Macmillan.

Kuykendall, E[lgin] V. 1954. *Eighty Years in the Changing West.* Pomeroy, WA (?): Privately printed.

Kuykendall, George Benson 1889. "A Graphic Account of the Religions or Mythology of the Indians of the Pacific Northwest, Including a History of Their Superstitions, Marriage Customs, Moral Ideas and Domestic Relations, and Their Conception of a Future State, and the Rehabiliment of the Dead." in *History of the Pacific Northwest: Oregon and Washington. . .,* ed. Elwood Evans II:60-95. Portland, OR: North Pacific History Company.

_____ 1919. *History of the Kuykendall Family Since Its Settlement in Dutch New York. . . .* Portland, OR: Kilham Stationery and Printing Co..

Laird, Carobeth 1980. "Chemehuevi Shamanism, Sorcery, and Charm," *Journal of California and Great Basin Anthropology* 2:80-87.

Larsell, Oloff 1947. "Medicine Among the Indians," in *The Doctor in Oregon, A Medical History.* Portland: Binfords & Mort (The Oregon Historical Society).

Lee, Irwin 1992. "Cherokee Healing; Myth, Dreams and Medicine," *American Indian Quarterly* 16:237-257.

Linton, Ralph 1923. *Annual Ceremony of the Pawnee Medicine Men.* Chicago: Field Museum of Natural History.

Lowie, Robert H. 1925. *A Trial of Shamans* in *American Indian Life*, Elsie Clews Parsons, ed. New York: B.W. Huebsch. See esp. pp. 41-43.

Lund, Astrid 1908. "Indiansk sagn digtning og de episke lawe," *Danske Studier* 5:175-188.

Maddox, John L. 1923. *The Medicine Man: A Sociological Study of the Character and Evolution of Shamanism.* New York: The Macmillan Co.

McWhorter, Lucullus Virgil 1940. *Yellow Wolf: His Own Story.* Caldwell, ID: The Caxton Printers, Ltd.

Moody, Raymond A. 1976. *Life After Life.* New York: Bantam Books.

Mooney, James 1896. *The Ghost-Dance Religion*, ARBAE 14:641-1110.

Washington, D.C.: Government Printing Office.

Morgan, William 1931. "Navaho Treatment of Sickness: Diagnosticians," *American Anthropologist* 33:390-402.

Murdock, George P. and Timothy J. O'Leary 1975. *Ethnographic Bibliography of North America*. 5 vols. 4th ed. New Haven: Human Relations Area Files Press.

————— 1965. "Tenino Shamanism," *Ethnology* 4:165-171.

Noll, Richard 1985. "Mental Imagery Cultivation as a Cultural Phenomenon: The Role of Visions in Shamanism," *Current Anthropology* 26:443-461.

Nomland, G.A. 1931. "A Bear River Shaman's Curative Dance," *American Anthropologist* 33:38-41.

Olrik, Axel 1965. "Epic Laws of Folk Narrative." Alan Dundes ed. *The Study of Folklore*, pp. 129-141. Englewood Cliffs, NJ: Prentice-Hall, Inc.

Opler, Morris E. 1935. "The Concept of Supernatural Power Among the Chiricahua and Mescalero Apaches," *American Anthropologist* 37:65-70.

————— 1943. "Navaho Shamanistic Practice Among the Jicarillo Apache," *New Mexico Anthropologist* (Albuquerque) 1:6-7, 16-18.

————— 1946. "The Creative Role of Shamanism in Mescalero Apache Mythology," *Journal of American Folklore* 59:268-281.

Park, Willard Z. 1933. "Paviotso Shamanism," *American Anthropologist* 35:98-113.

————— 1938. *Shamanism in Western North America: A Study in Cultural Relationships*, Northwestern University Studies in the Social Sciences 2. Evanston: Northwestern University.

Pepper, G.H. 1905. "An Unusual Navaho Medicine Ceremony," *Southern Workman* 34:228-235.

Rawlings, Maurice S. 1978. *Beyond Death's Door*. New York: Bantam Books.

Reichard, Gladys A. 1939. *Navaho Medicine Man, Sandpainting and Legends of Miguelito*. New York: J. J. Augustin.

Rogers, Spencer L. 1942. "The Methods, Results, and Values of Shamanistic

Therapy," *Ciba Symposia* 4: 1215-1224.

———— 1942. "Primitive Theories of Disease," *Ciba Symposia* 4:1190-1201.

———— 1942. "Shamans and Medicine Men," *Ciba Symposia* 4:1202-1214.

Sapir, Edward 1907. "Religious Ideas of the Takelma Indians of Southwestern Oregon," *Journal of American Folklore* 20:33-49.

———— 1909. *Wishram Texts, Together with Wasco Tales and Myths* [Collected by Jeremiah Curtin and Edited by Edward Sapir.] II: PAES. Leyden: E.J. Brill.

Schuster, Helen H. 1982. *The Yakimas: A Critical Bibliography.* Bloomington, Ind: Indiana University Press.

Siskin, Edgar E. 1983. *Washo Shamans and Peyotists; Religious Conflict in An American Indian Tribe.* Salt Lake City: University of Utah Press.

Smith, M.W. 1954. "Shamanism in the Shaker Religion of Northwest America," *Man* 54:119-122.

Spier, Leslie 1935. *The Prophet Dance of the Northwest and Its Derivatives: The Source of the Ghost Dance*, General Series in Anthropology 1. Menasha, Wi.: George Banta.

———— & Edward Sapir 1930. *Wishram Ethnography*, UWPA 3 No. 3:151-300. Seattle: University of Washington Press. See especially "Religious Practices and Beliefs," pp. 236-248.

Thompson, Stith 1946. *The Folktale.* New York: The Dryden Press.

———— 1955-58. *Motif-Index of Folk-Literature. . .* , 6 vols. Bloomington, IN: Indiana University Press.

———— 1966. *Tales of the North American Indian.* Bloomington, IN: Indiana University Press.

Walker, Deward E. Jr 1967b. "Nez Perce Sorcery," *Ethnology* 6:66-96.

———— 1970. "Sorcery Among the Nez Perces," in *Systems of North American Witchcraft and Sorcery*, D.E. Walker Jr. ed., pp. 267-295. Moscow: University of Idaho [Anthropological Monographs No. 1].

———— 1989. *Witchcraft and Sorcery of the American Native Peoples.*

Moscow: University of Idaho Press.

Wilson, S.C. and T.X. Barber, 1981. "Vivid Fantasy and Hallucinatory Abilities in the Life Histories of Excellent Hypnotic Subjects ("Sonambules"): Preliminary Report with Female Subjects,"in *Imagery: Concepts, Results, and Applications*, ed. E. Klinger. New York: Plenum Press.

_____ 1982. "The Fantasy-Prone Personaltiy: Implications for Understanding Imagery, Hypnosis, and Parapsychological Phenomena," in *Imagery: Current Theory, Research, and Applications*, ed. A. Sheikh. New York: Wiley.

Wyman, Leland C. 1936. "Navaho Diagnosticians," *American Anthropologist* 38:235-246.

Yellowtail, Thomas 1991. *Yellowtail: Crow Medicine Man and Sun Dance Chief, An Autobiography* (As Told to Michael Oren Fitzgerald.) Norman: University of Oklahoma Press.Biblio. pp. 237-239.

ACKNOWLEDGEMENTS

A. I am grateful to Mr. John Guido, Head, Manuscripts, Archives and Special Collections, Holland Library, at Washington State University, for permissions to publish manuscript portions of this volume and photographs.

B. I am especially grateful for the helpful reading of this manuscript by Judy McWhorter Goodwin together with her recollections of her grandfather, Lucullus V. McWhorter.

C. I am grateful to the Office of Printing and Photographic Services, Smithsonian Institution, for permission to publish the photograph of Sapan-wuxit, Yakima doctor—(Click Relander photo 1900).

D. The book's cover is by Starr Design, 7123 W Weaver Pl, Littleton, CO 80123. A traditional Wishram design depicts the protruding fangs of the rattlesnake.

E. And not least, I am grateful to Linda and to Alan for sharp-eyed proofreading. Remaining infelicities are all mine.

ORDER FORM

Great Eagle Publishing Inc.
3020 Issaquah–Pine Lake Rd. SE, Suite 481
Issaquah, Washington 98027-7255
FAX 206 391-7812

Please send:

_____ copies of **MAGIC IN THE MOUNTAINS, THE YAKIMA SHAMAN: POWER & PRACTICE** at $17.95 per copy.

_____ copies of **GHOST VOICES, YAKIMA INDIAN MYTHS, LEGENDS, HUMOR And HUNTING STORIES** at $23.95 per copy.

_____ copies of **THE FORGOTTEN TRIBES, ORAL TALES OF THE TENINOS AND ADJACENT MID-COLUMBIA RIVER INDIAN NATIONS** at $10.95 per copy.

I understand that I may return any book for a full refund—for any reason, no questions asked.

Name _____

Address _____

_____

City _____ State _____ ZIP _____

Phone (___) _____

Sales Tax
Add 8.2% for books shipped
to Washington State addresses.

Shipping
Book Rate: $1.75 for the first book
and $0.75 for each additional book
(Surface shipping may take three or four weeks)

Please photocopy this order form